Soul Reunion

The Return Home From Separation

Susann Taylor Shier

VELVET SPRING PRESS

Velvet Spring Press
Boulder, Colorado
www.VelvetSpringPress.com

ISBN-10 0-9771232-4-3
ISBN-13 978-0-9771232-4-7
Copyright information available upon request.

Cover Design: Manjari Graphics
Photograph on back cover by Jim Barbour
Interior Design: J. L. Saloff
Typography: Bembo

v. 1.0
First Edition, 2011
Printed on acid free paper.

Every breath is an intimate romance

with all that is beloved.

Susann

Contents

Part One:
Connection: The Way Home

PART TWO:
SOUL REUNION

6. BEYOND SEPARATION TO THE ULTIMATE FRONTIER 85

ACKNOWLEDGEMENTS

This book came to life through the generosity of Spirit. The nature and content of the words and sensation of sacred union with love given expression through this book for you to experience came from the wisdom, genious, Love and abiding presence of Spirit coming through me to my hands and pen and ink. If I were to give the collective of Spirit that brought to my heart and consciousness a title it would be, the Beloveds. I must first and foremost give thanks and honor to the realm of Spirit that created this book.

No less important is the invaluable team that once again came forward to let this magnificent creation of Spirit be in a form for you to relish. I treasure my team that has been with me for my trilogy of books, of which *Soul Reunion* is the third book.

To John Kadlecek, masterful editor and priceless contribution of excellence to my whole process of being a writer and author, I hold a place of deepest gratitude. Thank you so much to Amy Bayless, faithful transcriber, who allowed my hand written words to come to type written life. Her loyalty and willing spirit are a gift of gold to me. To Scarlett Joy, my assistant, who buoyantly filled in wondrous aspects of skill and enthusiasm to keep the project moving forward. Thank you Manjari Henderson for the brilliance of our co-creation of another fabulous book cover. To Jim Barbour and his skill in drawing forth my photographic best for the back cover. Once again, Sharon Garner proved herself invaluable as a precision copy editor and Jamie Saloff gave beauty and polish of design effortlessly.

So many friends gave loving support and encouragement to this creative endeavor which I found myself compelled to birth. I couldn't have done any of this without feeling the community of Love being held by them, that further opened my sacred heart to Love's words.

I must include mention of a special book, *Love Without End*, by Glenda Green, was instrumental in opening my understanding of, and connection with the exquisite majesty of the sacred heart that I describe in the book.

And to you, dear reader, my heart and soul shines brightly to know you through our connectedness as you relish your experience of sacred union in your journey out of separation home. Thank you for the magnification of sacred embodiment of Spirit you bring through your life.

Clients whose session content are described in the book gave full permission to me to use their material. It has been altered slightly in description to be easily readable for you. Client names have been changed to protect their identities.

PREFACE

The only wound is the wound of separation. We have heard this statement for years and it has made sense intellectually. Now, through the pages, and supportive energies of this book, you have the opportunity to heal this wound. The wound of separation reveals itself to you continually through your fears, struggles, stresses and sense of limitation. You feel it through your physical pains and illnesses. You feel it when your heart grieves for the lack of knowing union with Spirit and the sense of home residing within you. We feel it collectively when we witness or participate in outer disasters.

You know that you don't want to be separated from the life force that propels your existence. You want to relinquish your wounds and the causes of those wounds. You have not fully known how to relinquish those wounds that have kept you from living from the place of spiritual union with the Divine.

Life is meant to be a spiritual experience. When you reunite those places in yourself that are disconnected from your soul and Spirit, you experience the ultimate spiritual experience and the only true one. You find this truth by reaching inside for your wholeness and divinity with all life. You find your true sense of meaning and purpose by reuniting your aspects of self that have been held in separation with your expanding sense of wholeness.

You are not meant to disconnect from your humanness in order to be spiritually connected. When you judge or reject aspects of our humanness you, in fact, actually prevent Spirit's influence in your life moving through those aspects of our humanness.

This is your time to allow your soul and Spirit to be your life's guidance system. Let this guidance system bring all you need to open your life to a place of assured stability. Through this book you are being given the tools to know how to birth your creative self into a greater sense of wholeness. You will learn how to know that every aspect of you, as well as the whole universe, is available to support your deep longing to know spiritual union.

I honor your courage to take a joy filled step toward living from the brightness that holds the dawning of your world born of wholeness. As you reunite in your heart and soul to your universal home and bring every facet of your human expression into union, you will truly know the homecoming of your spirit embodied. This is your sacred fulfillment.

INTRODUCTION

The body has done a remarkable job of sustaining its vibrancy and well-being in spite of what appears to be our undying proclivity to separate from our soul's guidance. We have become masterful in using our capacity for free choice to make our own decisions outside of our connection to Spirit. In spite of this proclivity, the amount of unconditional grace our divine nature gives us is something to be deeply grateful for.

Your soul chose to come here to experience a physical reality. Your soul chose to create a body to give it a means to have an experience of the six senses and to know aliveness in the physical dimension.

The movie *City of Angels* was an excellent depiction of the nature of each one's soul journey here. Whether you saw the movie or not, your journey here started with the distinct choice to have the sensation of physical life. We all chose to step into the shoes of a human form communing with infinite Spirit. We said yes to this experience of consciously creating through the six senses moving in the physical capacity for expression. Your body longs to be unified with your soul so that you can have the greatest fulfillment possible of this physical experience called life.

Our body, as a vehicle for physical, mental and emotional expression, is longing to know Spirit's movement through it again and be reunited with the universal life source that gave birth to us. It is continually regenerating itself to give us renewed possibility to know wholeness in all ways possible.

The marriage of body and soul is a primary life purpose for each of us. And it is the only way for us to truly know divine fulfillment.

There are two routes to take to experience union of body and soul. First, your body and consciousness must awaken to receive Spirit's revelation as your guiding light. Second, the soul must honor the physical experience it has chosen.

In the first instance, separation occurs because we deny Spirit's gifts. In the second instance, separation is known when we try to live a spiritual life which is not embodied. We keep our spiritual wealth in an energetic realm when we enter higher states in ourselves, leaving our body, mind and heart high and dry from being engaged in this energetic wealth we touch. This occurs in times of heightened states of meditation that take us to euphoric states, or bring us grand visions that we are lost to implement. This also occurs in moments of disregard for our physical expression, or when we act from unconscious patterns of withholding from fully engaging in life here, for numerous reasons I will touch on later.

The body, in and of itself without a conscious spiritual connection, prefers comfort and protection. It is resistant to change and anything out of its structural comfort zone for maintaining a survival-based existence.

The soul is the adventurer and risktaker. It came to this realm of physicality for the adventure of physical life. It already knew how to be a soul being. This state is captured by the image of an angel plucking on the universal harp. It is the soul that loves the infinite field of physical experiences that provide endless possibilities for creation and play. It is the soul that guides us to experience what the capacity for physical and feeling sensation brings, the endless joys of being alive in a body: dancing, singing, smelling flowers, eating fine cuisine, seeing sights of exquisite beauty, knowing the full range of sensation in lovemaking, and on and on.

Our consciousness has lost its lighthouse of Spirit in attempting to navigate the complexities of human existence. The fact is, our lives only become complex and stress filled when our internal compass is not unified with Spirit. A human void of connection to Love will choose overprotection or destruction, such as greed, fear or manipulation, as its guide. This choice brings about the state of living beyond our means on all levels.

Soul reunion is the union of our capacity to know physical aliveness with our soul gifts and strengths. As our soul gifts find space in us, first in our sacred heart and then into the rest of our capacities, we awaken to the true enlightened state of being in Love with life itself. We discover the joy of igniting creation through our abundant means for its revelation through human form.

The Wound of Separation

I have held the premise that the only wound is the wound of separation for as long as I can remember. It is a premise that put me on a path to learn to live from my heart and soul. It is a premise that spoke to me of the chasm we experience between our magnificent, eternal nature filled with the Divine and the thin layers of human consciousness that insists on living outside of that place of splendor and purpose.

I have spoken in presentations, to clients, and even to people on the street for many years from my conviction that the only wound is the wound of separation. For sixteen years of working with clients, I have based my practice as a psychotherapist and intuitive counselor on it. As a psychotherapist I have studied a plethora of modalities for healing and incorporated a number of them. Every year, numerous new modalities come along to speed up, deepen and create more lasting results in our transformative journey to effectively handle these wounds of separation.

Throughout all of the tremendous advancements I have seen in the many ways developed to assist us to wholeness and health I have continually explored the role of our spiritual component in healing, recovery and returning to wholeness. I have always emphasized to clients in my intuitive counseling and psychotherapy practice to stop focusing on the lack, limitation or wound, and seek the resources and the qualities of Spirit needed to reclaim life where it was missing. My mission is to guide each one to reunite with the spiritual resources that they hold connection to as a means of healing this wound of separation.

This revelation of separation shows itself through every form of physical limitation, emotional lack of well-being and mental instability in our inability to create meaningful purpose in our working life, in our inability to Love and know intimacy, to know the spiritual fulfillment inherent in a state of wholeness, connection and a sense of oneness with divine purpose.

We are spiritual beings using the human dimension for spirit's expression. For too long we have not known how to be that. We have sought spiritual connectedness, but felt very inept at bringing that majestic, satisfying state into our daily existence.

I love to help build that bridge and teach people how to simply and effectively let every aspect of them that has been held out from being spiritually connected to life move back into union with Spirit so it may move through the heart and soul into every part of the experience of life.

What if all our discordant feelings were seen as beloved aspects of ourselves, trying to find their way home to be in reunion with our soul and all of creation? What if all our physical limitations were seen as beloved aspects of us crying out to be reunited with the life force they need to function as an extension of our spiritual capacity for expression?

As I am writing this book, we as a world are in the challenge of a recession. This is a spiritual matter. This potent time is very much a global picture revealing the dire consequence of living based on separation. This reflection of our internal state of separation is coming out into the external world for the purpose of rectifying it. That is the good news.

In this challenging time, we can see how light has been shed on the incredible degree of living beyond our financial means. In the United States, we believed we could draw on the whole world, through monies lent to us, to support our habit of living beyond our means.

This pattern relates directly to our lifestyle of separation. When we work as an individual with a personal will, based on what we imagine we must have to live the life we think we need to be happy, we are living beyond our connection to our spiritual resources. We are completely operating outside the realm of cocreation with Spirit. All we have is willpower, generated self-importance and "every man for himself" mentality. In this scenario, Spirit's influence is nowhere to be found.

We could put a majority of blame on the systems of this world for creating the outer evidence of our collective pattern of separation. That's easy. Or we could look at the ways that we have lived outside the realm of connection to all that is operating, very successfully, throughout our universe, galaxy and beyond. It is magnificent and magical to say the least.

When we live in the realm of disconnection we are always seeking outside sources of connection to power, joy and wholeness. For instance, purchasing something, whether it's a new home or a pair of shoes, can be a momentary high of power and delight. It can give us a feeling of instant gratification. We often will continue to acquire material items or accrue experiences to tap into our natural desire of being much larger or more expanded than we currently feel ourselves to be. As we have seen, this way of living has created recession, not expansion.

Vicarious living through the fuel of outside resources isn't enough anymore. To know fullness in our outer world we must create it first in ourselves. For us to truly feel our inner sense of wealth and abundance we must first get connected to the field of creation that is brimming with opportunities for creating anything we choose. That is what happens when we work *with* the universal laws of creation. They work for us. When we choose instant gratification we are not listening to our heart and soul, which are the doorway to a deeper sense of fulfillment to any desire or craving. It is time to focus on wanting what satisfies the heart's connection to a deeper sense of self.

It is time to validate the call of our soul and our heart.

First, we simply have to claim that the struggling aspects of our life are the result of buying in to patterns of separation from Spirit. Next we get in touch with that part of us that is experiencing the disconnection and get it reconnected. Then wholeness prevails, our life expands and our ability to be joyfully alive magnifies. This is what *Soul Reunion, The Return Home From Separation* is all about.

Throughout the book, as I speak of connection and soul union, I will use a variety of words to describe the field that we are connecting to and reuniting with. I call it a field because, in essence, it exists everywhere, other than the places where separation from that field have been chosen, or where the lack of connection to that field is being engaged in and held to, or reinforced. This field is a universal dimension of Spirit. It has many names and ways of being described. The key is our connection to this field in the way that is real and sacred to us. Focus on your experience of what it means to unite with all that is divine and let that experience flourish as you make the return home from separation.

Whether it is the universe, the All That Is, the Beloved, Love, the Divine, God, Creator, the field of creation—all are descriptions of that space that holds light and wholeness, unity and oneness. We are all of that. The universe sees us as its Beloved. Our embodiment of all of this field through reunion with it is our soul and life purpose.

The ultimate relationship is with the universe within us.

Let us take the next step together, discovering the how–to of soul reunion. It takes courage to face the pain of separation that is at the root of all pain, whether it is physical, emotional or soul-level pain. This courage is essential if we are to truly know our self and purpose, which our heart and soul, and all of life itself, is encouraging us to deeply know and revel in.

We feel the pull to our greatness continually. This pull is rooted in a universal support system, present and available continually. As we really grasp this and know this in our heart, embracing the facets of separation within us is not only doable but enjoyable. We can remember there is always a sensation of light present in the midst of our momentary dimness of pain or feeling of limitation.

When each of us as a soul came here we agreed to bring our soul gifts and our connection to the beloved universe of creation to this world. Part of the agreement in coming here was to assist in a collective reunion with Spirit. The people here were held in such a collective pattern of separation from Source, that our presence was called for to assist this world to come home to its original blueprint of soul union known through the body, mind and heart.

We committed to the universe that our mission here is to "go big or go home." Bring the connection to Love or move on. To go big is to live from Love, take the high road, and bring the inspiration of what it looks like and feels like to live in union with Love and the field of all of creation. That is our divine purpose.

I was the minister at a couple's wedding a number of years ago. Their motto for their reason to get married was "go big or go home." Their vow was their desire to "go big." That's such a fantastic creative purpose and challenge for saying, "I do," and committing oneself to deepen one's engagement in life through marriage.

It is the same for each of us in being born into this magnificent land called planet Earth. Our desire to be spiritual beings in a physical body has brought us to the point of declaring that it is time for us to make a vow to ourselves as we did with the universe, to embody Spirit and live in the land of "go big" which represents wholeness of connection in life, to be wildly plugged in and living the fullness of the soul's majesty.

My job with you now is to make this process easy and rewarding for you, so that knowing the sensation of soul reunion becomes as natural as breathing. It is my honor and pleasure to open the gates to a myriad of ways for you to have the means, the tools, and all the support you need in every dimension to know a life guided by your union with your soul and all of creation. I am offering a road map, or blueprint, but the voyage on the ship of life is uniquely yours. The journey from separation to fulfillment shines with Love, magic and power every step of the way.

As you read this book, the aspects of you that are longing and ready to be reunited to your beloved soul and Spirit will leap to the forefront to make it easy for you to give those parts what they are looking for. The more of you that knows reunion and is freed from the bondage of separation, the happier and more fulfilled you will be.

This book works on numerous levels. It can awaken many places in you that have only known separation. It can give you "aha!" moments of understanding how you have held yourself hostage to the isolation of separation. It will allow you to open those disconnected places that are ready to be reunited with Spirit. It will ignite the flame of life in you again where you didn't even know it had been extinguished. It will bring in light where you never imagined you could truly know light again. You can heal the wounds once and for all that have kept you from being the brilliant many-faceted jewel of infinite Love that you are. It will give you full permission and the know-how to be the magnificent creator that you know in your heart and soul that you are.

The return home from separation takes us to the only true place of security: the joy of experiencing union with infinite Love, in our sacred heart and fullness of being—this is truly knowing home.

Your reunion with all that is beloved is the greatest Love story ever known. This is your story. May you revel in it; may you experience the sacred treasure that is you.

Part One:

Connection:
The Way Home

1

THE WEALTH OF CONNECTION

There is a cosmic song in a resonant field of creation continually playing. Under the influence of this resonant field of Love, life can be created as a string of notes effortlessly emerging. Connection to this cosmic song is soul reunion.

Your radiance acts as a beacon, drawing the abundance of the universe to you.

What does soul reunion look like?

What does it feel like?

How will I know I am in that space of union?

If connection is the means for knowing soul union, what am I connecting to?

Where is it and how do I get it?

These are the questions that will be answered as you travel through the pages of this book and let yourself receive the gift of connection and reunion.

You are a grand soul. Now is your chance to finally embody not just your potential, but your largest dreams. The process is quite simple, once you learn the basic mechanics of it. You get to be your authentic, free-Spirited self that knows that Love is what you want to know in every part of yourself and your life.

First of all, I encourage you to ask yourself what you truly want to experience when you feel the longing, in any moment, to be connected. Wanting to be more fully connected lets us know that aspects of us are not feeling connected, and that is why we have the longing. These aspects are standing up to be counted. They are proclaiming their readiness to get on board our "soul ship" to reunite with the juice of creation, so that they may function as part of our wholeness of expression, not outside of it.

Wanting to be more fully connected and in union with Spirit is the most natural creative impulse there is, outside of breathing.

Breathing our purpose in coming here is to bring the universal field of Love and creation to this world we call planet Earth. So it is very appropriate that we wish to be experiencing the wholeness of Love and creation not just in theory, but fully within ourselves, so it may pulsate into this world. As we live in union with creation we become the transformational agents, working on behalf of the Divine, that we know we are designed to be.

What would your life be like if you never had to experience separation from your divine source? What if you held that connection deeply and completely within your being? What if you explored the bounty of creation with the lighthouse for Love intact and held sacred within you? How would your life, your soul's journey, be different?

The Look of Connection

Defining connection for your self is paramount. How will you feel when you are connected? Will you be filled with Love, strength, freedom or purposeful expansiveness? It is vital to know what is valuable to you. And this can always change.

Our experience of connection is ever-expanding.

To be connected to Spirit we are not meant to be perfectly still and connect to one small point in the universe as though we are hitting the middle circle of a large target with our bow and arrow. Connection, to be real, is a connection to the field of all creation. It continually expands and accumulates wealth, wisdom and eternal and limitless qualities of experience.

Spiritual connection is a connection to the field of creation that holds limitless possibilities for creative expression through us. This connection we wish for will be limited if we see connection merely as a silver thread to God, as a finite source of existence.

Soul reunion to the beloved universal wholeness includes every quality of Spirit imaginable, and then some. It opens magnificence, splendor, supreme Love and so much more beyond what is nameable.

Creative Vulnerability

To connect requires creative vulnerability in the land of the unknown, which is merely the creative void. Our openness and movement into the creative void is essential to reunite with the vastness and sacredness of holy communion with Spirit in our lives.

The vastness of creation is continually playing a symphony that magnifies the celebration of connection and union everywhere. There is just a thin layer of human consciousness and the physical dimension being held out in separation from that symphony of creation. You are utterly supported by all creation in your journey from separation to fulfillment in every nanosecond. This universal gift of union with the beloved All That Is pours over you and through you, eternally, as you are open in creative vulnerability to it.

Receptor Sites

It is our development of energetic receptor sites within our human dimension that is paramount to our embodiment of our soul. Receptor sites are energetic places in our body, mind and heart that are available for receiving Spirit in all its qualities and facets. The chakras are well-known examples of energetic receptor sites. In many cultures it is said that we have hundreds of chakras throughout our body. This increase in receptor sites provides a broader field for creation within us, so we are in union with the universal field of creation our soul knows so well. Our soul has *never* forgotten this union. But our human dimension, which our souls created to give Spirit expression, combined with our right of free choice, has caused separation from that field. This is our time to reunite our human dimension with Spirit by allowing all that we are to be receptor sites for the design of life being held so majestically in this universe we value, waiting for our invitation for connection within all available aspects of our expression.

Our heart, mind and body are a dwelling place for Spirit's conveyance, to the degree that we reunite the places in us that have separated from Spirit's wealth. We can receive Spirit in exact proportion to the amount of space we hold available to the universal breath of infinite Love. As we heal the wound of separation held in various aspects of ourselves, we open more receptor sites for the infusion of Love within us. When we move out of disconnection into connection, these receptor sites light up. Our wiring evolves to its original place of union and synchronization, and a greater sense of wholeness is felt. This is one of the many ways to describe how we might feel in our body when we are reunited with infinite presence.

Soul Embodiment

In essence, we are stating, "Into thy hands, field of all creation, I command my life movement." This includes my heart and every aspect of me I have held out of the realm of Spirit that I may cocreate again in wholeness. Then "thy hands" includes "my hands."

This soul embodiment is our personal and universal fulfillment. There is no separation between our fulfillment and the cosmic fulfillment. It is not selfish to prioritize your connection and soul embodiment in your life. This is how you serve and transform in this world. You only radiate what is authentically yours. You can't give what you don't have. When we give from the place of disconnection, we are operating out of hidden personal will. That never satisfies. It is this personal will that created separation in the first place. A personal will is always born of separation. We are in separation, motivated by the sentiment, "What's in this for me?" This is an ego-based act. Embodiment of true purpose asks what the will of the heart and soul is in each moment.

Soul embodiment is the most authentic gift we have to offer. We share it through its natural outpouring. As we embody the field of infinite Love, creation and true power, it is contagious. We live a soul-directed life when we are embodied from a soul level.

For instance, our lack of direction in a given area of our life is a direct result of the separation from our true compass, our North Star. That guidance is effortless when we are in union with Spirit in mind and heart. When we are open to receive divine guidance, we are in cocreation with Spirit. Divine guidance does not work in spite of us; it works because of us. It acts as a fluid reality because all of our receptor sites are open to Spirit. That is always a choice.

As divine guidance orchestrates our life movement we can't wait to see how the symphony of our life is written and created. The symphony is made up of every facet of us, from our energy field to every atom and particle of DNA. We are not just hoping and praying for Spirit's guidance, we know, as a cocreator, that Spirit is our symphonic conductor and the field of all of creation is the stage we play on. The world then reflects our abundance of connection in all ways.

As a client once said to me, "I can't imagine being on Earth at this time *without* sacred connection to my soul and my spiritual home and family. I wouldn't dare leave home without it."

Union

Our primary relationship is with Spirit, with Love. Our primary purpose is to heal the wound of separation, wherever it arises in us, so our relationship with Spirit can be expressed through the brightness and clarity of our life. True success comes from successful union with the beloved All That Is. Each moment is our opportunity to create a greater, more profound and satisfying relationship with the universal dance of life. It may appear that true success comes from monetary wealth or a perfect marriage or family life, but we know increasingly that this just isn't so. As we truly reunite with the beloved All That Is, we have a menu of infinite possibilities for successful orchestration of creation through us. It just might include monetary wealth, or family bliss. When we act from the place of union, these elements of success feel fulfilling to us because our heart and soul have ignited them, not our drive to survive or be powerful in our personal agenda born of separation from Source.

In each moment there is the opportunity to expand our knowing of divine connection, as we heal the wound of separation. It is our choice to determine what we will be in relationship with: divinity or fear. When we choose fear we perpetuate the many faces of separation within us.

If we focus our attention on someone or something outside ourselves as our primary relationship, we are asking that person or belief system to play God to us and our existence. This could refer to a person, a religion, a political system or any perceived outside source of power for us. In these ways, we have deliberately separated from our divine source and its guidance. We are choosing to separate from our inner union with Spirit and let "other" be our guidance system or True North. It is that simple. In each moment we choose what our first love is. When we choose connection to infinite Love as our starting point, we are blessed with the reflection that appears through an abundance of love-filled creative relationships in our life.

As we move out of our self-created patterns of separation and fearlessly cocreate with the Beloved as our life partner, our heart is guided by this true compass. We can then create from our heart, filled with beloved connection to others. The game of playing God to others, or letting others play God to us, is up. It simply dissolves because we choose a larger, more authentic relationship that will never abandon, reject or betray us.

Here is a simple, sacred way to know divine connection and soul reunion in this moment. You can say the following words out loud or to yourself:

> *Beloved, I am totally yours in these moments in heart and soul, as I hold a sacred knowing in every aspect of me that we are cocreating a grand universal symphony that I feel a deep joy and privilege to be part of. I know I am held in the infinite presence of the Creator and my connection to that presence is not only intact but guides my sacred heart, igniting my passion for life. Our union is Love; our Love song is an unchained melody resounding through my body, as the body we share: The Beloved.*
>
> *I know my purpose and contributions are profound for my soul is infused with Love and I feel the honor of living in union with this beloved All That Is that I am. It is a privilege to connect with the beauty of creation and the essential joy that is life.*

Knowing Soul Reunion

There is an eternal dialogue happening between you and that one Spirit of the All That Is. It is an eternal breath, always pulsating, and you are a never-ending, unique expression of this eternal breath. There is no separation in this essence place. This essence place within you where there is connection to the eternal dialogue can always be touched and tapped into. Within this eternal dialog is an eternal ocean of resources. How could we ever be concerned with running out of resources?

The exploration for you is the discovery of what connection and union looks and feels like for you. It is unique for you. It is also ever-expanding, so its look and feel may change.

**Our experience of connection is not meant
to be unchanging.**

As we integrate more of our separate, lost self, we expand our capacity within us to know the majestic nature of soul connection. We move beyond the need to be healed, to the place of purpose in simply magnifying Love and creation through us.

Connection is known through experiencing union with qualities of Spirit. When we know these qualities of Spirit, resounding as notes of a celestial symphony within us, we feel expanded and open while feeling anchored to a sense of authentic security at the same time. This is the look and feel of the embodiment of Spirit. Soul embodiment is the key ingredient to dissolving aspects of separation within us.

Healing the wound of separation takes place though the simple process of displacement or replacement. As we embody soulful dimensions of Spirit's resources, the patterns of separation simply fall away. Our cells can only hold one thing at a time. It is what we value most that will be held, be it joy or fear. So, as we embody qualities of our Spirit, such as joy, the patterns of separation naturally dissolve in the light of joy, and easily let go to being replaced by our first Love. In this instance, that is joy over fear.

Connection is Limitless

Our heart and soul union with Spirit may feel deeply satisfying or buoyant and joyful. We may feel more "solidly" present or light as a feather. There are a myriad of facets to the experience of connection. Do not limit yourself to how soul union feels. As more aspects of you come into union with the Divine, you blossom and grow. Your capacity to be a container for universal pulsation expands and strengthens. The look of connection may vary. However, the key ingredient is a sense of knowing, and coherence through heart and soul and body, that eternal life not only prevails but flourishes in you.

Coherence in the human dimension comes when union with our soul and the resonant field of all creation is creative and alive. It is so much more than a spacey state that you might consider to be spiritual. A spacey, albeit blissful, state of being out of the body is in fact a state of disconnection. We might feel expanded in our awareness, but our body is not engaged with the spiritual bliss being experienced. As we develop increased receptor sites in ourselves for the light of Spirit, we feel the coherence of connection in our body, mind and heart. It is not spacey nor does it exist merely in our higher awareness. It lives in us. Thus, soul fulfillment comes as a deeper, richer, expanded union that is known with all of creation.

The Collective True North

We are at a pivotal point in history in assisting this world to know a collective pattern of soul reunion. I call it reinstating or returning to the original blueprint for the Earth.

Many issues that are coming up now for all of us feel ancient. They are, in fact. They must come up to be cleared and transformed so that the gold in the wound of separation is mined and planetary oneness and wholeness follows.

There is a collective sense that we have lost our inner compass of True North and don't know what or whom to trust. In the space of separation, we should be wary of what is trustworthy. Our only job right now is to reclaim True North in ourselves, for ourselves. From this perspective we know what we can trust and what is not worthy of our trust.

Currently there is also a collective trauma around the feeling that the world might end. This brings up all our traumas from past lives around the deaths we have had. Having these traumas stirred magnifies the fears of the world ending tenfold. Certainly the world based largely on our patterns of separation is due to end. It is in the process of ending right now. As we let go of our patterns of separation and reclaim our value in our connection to True North, we will tangibly feel our union with everlasting life. As each of us reconnects with that universal perspective of everlasting life, we actually begin to recreate our world, personally and then collectively. It is exciting to see and be part of this new world emerging out of our union with the field of all creation.

We can open to welcoming the Divine into every aspect of our life. Ask for this eternal resource. This is a way of declaring that we want partnership with the Divine. We create it as our primary relationship and guiding light. Allowing ourselves to know union with our primary relationship with the symphonic nature of the Divine allows us to be in union with the field of true Love in all our relationships.

Let yourself be received into the arms of Spirit. It always receives you. It celebrates your connection. And let yourself celebrate your connection. The more you relish, celebrate, give thanks for and make sacred your union with beloved Spirit, the more space you create for its infusion in you.

2

THE SACRED HEART

Beloved union is first experienced in the sacred chamber of our inner hearts. This sacred heart within us has never been disconnected from Spirit. The sacred heart, in its pristine nature, is the one space for connection with our Creator which has always been provided, no matter what our physical, mental or emotional state. And we were never able to sever this connection even if we participated in causing separation within various other aspects of our human capacity.

This pristine space belonging to the Divine is the space where union between our divine connection and our human dimensions come together. The human heart is intended to be the conduit for Love's movement through the sacred heart to the physical dimension. In healing the wound of separation you will bring those parts of you feeling lack, limitation, emptiness and struggle to this beautiful space of the sacred heart where those parts may join with infinite Spirit and Love. Then you will connect your sacred heart with your human heart so Love can pulse through your very bloodstream. You will place your pictures, images, impressions, sensations, colors, sounds and knowledge of what divine connection is like for you in your sacred heart so those separate parts may be held and embraced in this receptor sight for Spirit's loving, assured infusion.

Infinite Love is known through our heart. It holds a place for the continuum of divine connection. As our sacred heart is allowed to expand within us to include more of its sacred, infinitely connected nature, we create a larger space for all those aspects of us that have been held in separation to come home through the heart to Love. The sacred heart holds a space for absolute connection to Source. In that sacred space we are forever able to connect to the Beloved, regardless of how far we have strayed.

The sacred heart carries the stillness we equate with the eye of the storm, where there is essential quiet. This is the realm of the incomprehensible and the great mystery that the sacred heart opens us to. The heart is not only still, but magnetic. Its magnetic quality generates all our life energy. It's like a resource station, especially since it is unequivocally connected to the field of all creation. For our Spirit to come through us, our heart must hold the place of home. It must be open and welcoming to our soul's movement and its connection to every resource of the universe. We can see how the heart is a vast generating plant and the power center for all our creation.

Within the sacred space of the heart is held our soul's deepest desires and purposes for coming to the Earth in the first place. The heart holds a generosity and nobility that is naturally an inspiration.

When you create from the sacred heart, which only knows unity with all that is, you create from Spirit. The resource field that is Spirit accesses the creative void of the vastness of yet unshaped life. We might have felt it as a great unknown, but to Spirit and the sacred heart, this vast reservoir is actually the known. It is the only field for creation that can be trusted from which to draw forth our creativity. So, when you are open in your heart to Spirit, you are actually creating from the known—from Spirit's perspective. This known you can trust.

Cultivating the heart's depth creates space to welcome the expanded field of all creation. The secret to manifestation always includes engaging our heart. This sacred heart is in the inner chamber of the heart. As Spirit moves through it, the heart becomes the chamber for Spirit's manifestation; when we connect our desires of the heart with Spirit, creating is certain.

The Felt Experience of Love

We know Spirit's voice as qualities of Spirit that evoke feeling sensations through us. As Love moves through the heart, you know it. The felt experience is not at all the same as the emotional realm. Our sacred heart does not carry our emotional responses. The sacred heart is an energetic space that always maintains connection to Spirit. Our human heart holds our felt experience of connection to infinite Love, as it is meant to. And we have also cluttered it with our emotional responses to our disconnection and separation to infinite Love.

Most often our emotions are counterproductive reactions to the feeling experiences of Spirit, moving through the sacred heart to our human heart into our bloodstream. For instance, Love pours radiantly through the heart and the emotion of fear may arise in response, blocking the manifestation of Love. Another example of emotional response to Love is grief. Grief comes in response to the desire for Love's presence. Grief is the emotion experienced due to the lack of feeling Love that had an impact on us at a previous time in our life. Both fear and grief dissolve when infinite Love fills the heart and naturally dissolves emotions that hallmark the lack of Love.

When you honor and rest in the sacred heart, its fire lights up and fuels all that you are in that moment. You come alive, fueled by a fresh supply of Spirit particles from an abundant universe. Spirit particles are life matter in the universe that activates all Love as creation for us to draw from in bringing Love into human experience. They are the smallest particle of energy available that forms the bridge between matter and Spirit. They are the flow of Love. For instance, you can stop a storm by loving it because the Spirit particles are affected and allow the "nonphysical" Love to impact the physical matter of the storm. There is no limit to the Spirit particles that can be drawn to you when you reside in your sacred heart. You begin to know what it is to move beyond healing to the transformative state of being available to infinite possibilities for creation. This experience moves into your human heart and into the bloodstream to feed your whole body with the message that I am infinite Love, creating from the field of infinite abundance.

True Openness of the Heart

True openness resides in the realm of the sacred. We are meant to be vulnerable and open to Spirit, not blindly open, to others and all that is around us. When we are vulnerable to Spirit, its magic and strength reside in us. We then hold a rich sense of knowing how to create freely from the security of our connected openness. Our connected openness of the sacred heart is the only true security. We are secure in knowing all that is of Spirit is within us. We sense how genuinely authentic and vulnerable we can be with those we relate to. Our vulnerability of the heart to Spirit's wisdom will accurately guide and inform us. We learn to hold a trust in our heart to hear Spirit's voice. That is a priceless gift to have and to hold.

The sacred heart is thus a powerful, holy space. It is the true space for prayer. True prayer is the communion of you and your Beloved, experienced in your sacred heart. In that chamber of beingness, all you have to do is enter and pray for the creation you long for. You magnify the birth of Love and light through the avenue of creation that is vital to you and your soul's beauty. As you are joined in this space of the sacred heart with All That Is, a power is activated which will attract whatever is real and needed.

The Heart as the Way Home

It is through the heart that we find our way home, including every aspect of us that has known separation. As we allow ourselves to see and know our sacred heart as the way home, all within us that is carried in separation can feel safe to return to this magnetic center of the Beloved within us. This is the space where spiritual reunion is known. So the sacred heart is not only the main receptor site for the infinite possibilities of Spirit being given life expression through us, but the sacred receptor site for all within us that has been held in separation to receive the wealth of Spirit again.

The heart truly is the seat of highest intelligence and the center of creativity. It connects us to the incomprehensible and the mystery. As we allow this state to be our truth, our physical, mental and emotional capacities will be effortlessly drawn, quite naturally, out of separation into the arms of Love, as our home ground.

We can see also how the heart is truly the center of health and well-being. As it goes in your heart, so it goes in your body. If your heart is flourishing in its expanded space of welcoming Love and the field of all creation, then it continually renews, revitalizes and magnifies life throughout the whole human dimension for Love's radiant expression.

It is the greatest transformer known within human existence. The heart changes, so does our entire experience of life. It is not a change of mind, but a change of heart that transforms us. Thoughts in and of themselves cannot make the essential difference. But thoughts, visions, dreams or possibilities birthed from the sacred heart catalyze real changes that truly serve our wholeness and expansion.

The heart is also the greatest problem-solver. Remember, you can't solve a problem at the level of the problem. It is our thoughts running through our mind that create our perceived problems. It takes change of heart, and the larger perspective of Spirit moving through the heart, to bring true clarity of direction, purpose, solution, resolve and, thus, new beginnings.

The greatest gift the sacred heart brings, as a cocreator with Spirit, is the treasure chest of inspiration. Inspiration by its very nature allows us to know that something that seems impossible can be done. The sacred heart is the source of an inspired life.

Cocreation through the Heart

Imagine that you are infinite and you can perceive infinite wealth and depth in your heart. You become the richness of the universe. You are in partnership as cocreator with the universe. You are here to extend infinity into the experiences of this dimension as light moving into life.

As cocreators, you and the universe made a covenant. This covenant makes it possible for you to have all the resources you need to make your life work.

It is when we become separated in our various ways from this covenant of cocreation that we let our mind, disconnected from the heart and the universal covenant, get us to think that we don't have what we need. In the space of separation that is a valid thought, because we don't have what we need when we are disconnected from life's resources. If we feel in any moment that we don't have what we need, we can be sure that we are experiencing separation. When you reside in the covenant of cocreation between you and the universe, your heart will be filled with the deep sense that you have all that you need.

The Seat of Love

Love moving through the sacred heart is the source of your life. As Love fills the sacred chamber of the heart, it brings a smile to your whole body.

Love is the power of the universe and the heart welcomes its presence into the experience of being human.

Because of Love moving in us we know a sense of oneness with Creator and all of creation. We feel as though we hold the same DNA with all the rest of the universe. As we commune with all of creation, Love becomes our family, our home.

Imagine yourself moving in a world in which Love as Spirit activates your human heart and is in the blood pumping through your veins to feed every organ, tissue and cell of your body. Imagine Love setting into motion all you create. This is the true blueprint for human life.

To Be in Love

Our heart is held within the universal heart. This universal heart holds the essence and space of true home. When we know this experience of communion within our sacred heart, between our self and the universal heart, we have truly discovered what it means to be in Love. We then allow ourselves to experience what it is to be one with the universal Beloved, which is our Beloved; to be in Love with all of creation and life itself. As we let ourselves commune with the universal heart, our home, we know the infinite nature of connection.

The Beloved is in Love with the essence of who we are.

Communion With Love

Communion with that which we love is as natural as breathing. We commune with that which we hold valuable every moment. Physically, if we love exercise, or fitness, for example, we will want to commune with that experience and engage in an activity that feeds that love of ours. If we love physical comfort we will seek the experience that produces comfort.

At the level of feeling, we may love or desire happiness and seek to commune with those situations that birth or breed happiness. If we value fear as a means of safety or protection, we will find ourselves communing with inner states or outer situations that fuel that fear.

As we hold sacred our connection to Love and the universal heart, we will be fed by its infinite Love and its resources that naturally activate our life. This is the natural Spirit of cocreation at play. This is the most expanded, abundant expression of Love there is.

Loving the Self

The greatest, most loving gift we can give ourselves is our reunion and communion with infinite Love. To be plugged in to all that Love is creates a home base, a receptor site for all those parts of us that have been held in separation from the Love that we are. We know we are Love when we allow our self the gift of communion with infinite Love. As we open this gift to all that we are, as consciousness creating in physicality, we allow our self to feel utterly, thoroughly, generously, filled with all that Love is.

The deepest form of self-love we can know is experienced when we extend infinite Love and Spirit to those parts of us that are struggling due to separation from what they are truly longing for. If you are existing outside of Love, what is the nature of the Love you have to give yourself when you work hard to experience self-love? It will not be a satisfying source of Love. It is much more productive and useful to bring those parts of you not feeling loved or lovable to the table of infinite Love and you will feast on the greatest cornucopia of nourishment possible. You will feel all those vacant, unexplored places in your self receiving the bounty of limitless, sacred, trustworthy Love.

> **Reunion and communion with divine Love takes us home, and is the greatest act of self-love there is.**

Our communion with divine Love brings us into union with the beloved All That Is. When this state imbues our cells, our fears and our weaknesses now have a safe haven that is trustworthy to come home to. Love moving through the sacred heart is the grand transformer. It holds a place for anything outside of it to be given the freedom, the choice, to once again know what it means to rest in the universal heart of home. Abandonment, betrayal, rejection will never have to be suffered again.

A heart filled with caretaking, nurturing love is a beautiful thing. But a heart that is only available to give caretaking love to others, and not available to receive and commune with divine Love, will ultimately suffer. If we are only living through caretaking love, we don't have the fuel of connection to the divine resources we need to provide a home base of Love within us to those parts of us that are suffering or frozen in fear and separation.

I spoke to a woman who was having an increasing feeling of anger toward her teenage sons, her husband and some of her coworkers. She had always been such a nice, easygoing person that her anger surprised and then scared her. She asked me what I thought might be going on that was evoking her seemingly unfounded anger. She had heard of the term "boundaries" and wondered if it was just a matter of having bad boundaries.

Her teenage sons were seventeen and nineteen, so she was moving into her years of empty nesting. It was her time to stop being primarily a caretaker. It was leaving her drained and exhausted instead of feeling loved and rewarded.

We did some deep work and she discovered that she was craving to know a connection to spiritually based Love, not just caretaking love. Her anger stemmed from a sense of powerlessness around her ability to have Love nurture her. It was always taking care of others and her heart and soul and cells were crying out for a richer experience that truly allowed her to feel like she was creating her world and relationships from divine Love. Caretaking love was leaving her feeling hollow and angry at her own choices.

As she reacquainted herself with her natural connection to divine Love, which subsequently filled her and radiated to her family and coworkers, she felt much lighter and brighter, not only in her heart but in all her relationships.

Communing first with divine Love and then letting that experience genuinely ignite our life is truly a fulfillment of purpose and our world at the same time.

> **The heart, open to universal Love, is the heart that knows the multifaceted expression of Love that physical existence has the privilege to experience.**

Our mission as a spiritual being with a human dimension is to keep the receptor sites of the sacred heart open to receive the universal heart's influence. The universal heart is the extension of our sacred heart in the universal dimension of existence. This universal heart holds the space for infinite Love for the human dimension. As we connect to the essence of infinite Love in our feelings we can know that the universal heart holds a sacred space for the knowing of infinite Love.

In the Spirit of cocreation you can remember that not only is the universe our Beloved, but the universe calls you its Beloved. When we take this statement into our heart and know we are beloved in the heart of the universe, we are filled with a sense of expanded Love for our self as an abundant aspect of all that is beloved.

Creating from Love

We can only truly create when we are in this space of the fullness of Love. When we hold ourselves sacred enough, as a spiritual being in a human capacity, to give ourselves the gift of reunion over and over again, we truly feel ourselves to be a creation in the vast field of all creation. It becomes a privilege to engage as the radiant expression of divine Love that we are. Our Spirit, fueled by communion with our sacred heart, ignites our life graciously and generously.

As creators coming from this holy place of the fullness of connection within us, we can now ask ourselves what we wish to cocreate with all of creation. As we live in soul Love we can now ask ourselves what our perspective is on every area of our life. We will be filled with the magic of how Love sees the world and how Love interacts with those places in us that have held separation through fear and suffering. Those separated aspects can now easily find this place of sacred Love being held in us, welcoming us home.

The Beloved is in Love with the essence of who we are.

3

The Heart:
True Love

The heart that we most commonly think of as the human heart, or the heart where we feel many emotions and sensations, is the heart we have created protection around, so we would not get hurt. The sacred heart holds our connection to infinite Love. The human heart is designed to be the extension of the sacred heart. It is the receptor site for experiencing Love at the human level.

The Guarded Human Heart

We bought into the idea, long ago or just recently, that closing the heart and walking in life with a guarded heart was the only way to survive. In one respect that is true. If we guard our heart, we can only survive. There is no room with a protected heart for the field of creation to move in us. Consequently, a closed-off heart does keep us from seeing a creator and keeps us merely surviving and maintaining in our life. A guarded or protected heart may seem essential to keep out "bad vibes," this crazy world, or all we perceive being harmful. The truth is that a guarded heart is not selective. Everything is kept from it. That includes the influence of infinite Love, the field of all creation and the universal support and strength that we are designed to live from.

The Will of the Heart

If the heart is infused with divine Love, it holds the greatest power there is. In that stance, there is nothing to guard against. We hold a natural inner barometer connected to Source that allows us to know what we can trust to let into our heart and what does not resonate with that sacred space. Our absolute connection to Spirit that we will not betray, no matter what, establishes in us an inner barometer of guidance to perceive and discern what course to take in any moment. From this space we are listening from the sacred heart, following the will of the heart. We can now feel fearless because the heart emanates its natural courage, which comes from its anchoring in the universal heart.

The Disconnected Heart

When the heart is closed to infinite Love, it is bound to feel a sense of loneliness, abandonment, betrayal or rejection. When any of these feeling states arise, the heart is telling us that it does truly feel separate from its source nourishment of infinite Love. This is a very natural way for it to communicate its sense of disconnection and subsequent longing to be reunited with the Beloved.

When the heart has become completely walled off, it doesn't even feel the urge to know reunion. Any degree of walling off of the heart's emanation can create all sorts of human heart patterns or problems. Be thankful to feel that sense of abandonment or loneliness. The key is to feed those parts longing to come out of the locked-down, guarded state of our own making, and to recognize what is being called for and to give these parts of our broken heart the infusion of Love they are asking for.

Love is revealed through its endless yearning to be known through us.

Longing for the expression of the multiple facets of Love in life is natural. That is one of the purposes we came to know and fulfill. It is vital to remember infinite Love, the richest nature of Love that we came to experience, first and above all else. Our communion with infinite Love is what allows us to be alive and receptive, and thus to experience the radiance of Love that we witness in the plant, animal and mineral kingdoms all around us.

Relationship Love

If we always keep our relationship with the Beloved primary, and our relationship of cocreation with others secondary, we will never be letting go of Love.

Every time you take yourself away from Love, recognize that this is the primary relationship you long for. When you say you want the Love a relationship gives you, you imagine that a relationship will give you unconditional Love, support, respect, adoration and full-on presence. Only if we bring these qualities of Spirit within us first can we find those qualities in a partner or intimate relationship. Sacred union with infinite Love is the one true relationship we can count on. It dwells within us, is connected to the universal heart of Love, and is ours forever.

From this place, a plethora of relationships infused with Love will birth themselves before you. All relationships hold within them a longing for connection to Love.

Masculine Presence as Love

For me, personally, I have noticed the natural pull toward wanting more outer representation of clear, conscious, connected male energy in my life. This can be reflected in intimate partnership, mentoring teachers or respected male friends in my life. The power of the presence of unwavering connection is the gift being sought through all those resources. As a woman, I don't believe I am alone in this desire to know clear, masculine energy more fully in my experience. This desire is true for men as well. It may show up for you men as the urgency for clarity, direction, purpose and confidence. All are masculine dimensions of Spirit.

What we are all truly seeking is to know and embody the truth of masculine energy which is the energy of absolute connection to Spirit. We long for it to be awakened in us more deeply and with greater assurance. As that occurs, we are then blessed to create in our world those clear reflections around us of this masculine energy we seek. This can take many forms of relationship. All are aspects of the dance of masculine and feminine dimensions of Love being personified within us and in our life.

If we don't hold this absolute connection to Spirit that masculine energy presents inside us, we will be inclined to mistrust masculine energy, push it away, put it down or reject it altogether as we play out these patterns of separation from absolute connection.

When our aspects are deprived of the strength of anchored presence that masculine energy in divine connection symbolizes, they shut down, give up and begin to create guarding, protecting mechanisms to justify their inability to create healthy, Love-filled outer relationships. These aspects can speak with great conviction and consequently override our natural longing to be absolutely connected to infinite Love no matter what. When we know connection to divine Love within us, this is the union of masculine and feminine energy within us rejoicing.

Trusting Masculine Love

When I hear a woman say she doesn't trust men, I gently remind her that it is not men she doesn't trust, but the masculine aspect of Spirit she doesn't trust. This stems from the fact that at some point in her soul journey she betrayed that connection and she now doesn't trust her ability to hold it. She has projected this loss onto the masculine, saying that men in general can't hold that connection, or will surely betray it.

The same will hold true of men who don't trust women. It is the feminine aspect of Spirit and Love that is not trusted, and that is an internal component for both men and women. Trusting masculine or feminine Love always starts on the inside.

If we keep our connection to infinite Love sacred and respected in ourselves, especially in our heart, we will trust Love and our divine union with it.

We are the ones who have hurt our hearts, been mean to our hearts, abandoned Love's place in our hearts. Anything else we proclaim about others causing the pains in our hearts is an excuse not to take responsibility to hold Love sacred and connected in ourselves.

What if you knew that Spirit's presence as Love was always here for you and you knew it was not going anywhere? This is the only security you can know. When you hold that inner security in Love, you will feel secure and taken care of in your life of Love.

If we are struggling in our relationship to another we are disconnected from our primary relationship to Spirit. This you can count on. There may be communication issues, power struggles or feeling-based issues to resolve, but without our connection to Love as our primary relationship, outer relationships will reflect this inner struggle and angst that actually stems from our primary disconnection and consequent suffering. This is a whole new way to look at relationship challenges, but certainly worth the exploration. To see how to live from the expanded space of infinite Love surely gives you an anchored, assured inner place that can handle all the volcanic, tumultuous events that come across our relational screen.

Letting Go to Love in the Field of Relationship

**All that you have ever created in connection to
Spirit and Love is yours forever.**

It is essential to claim this truth for yourself whenever you feel you
are losing someone or something. It is not a time to create more separation from the connection to Love, even though it may feel like Love is
leaving you. It is not Love that is leaving you. You have equated your
experience of Love with the other person's presence. You think that
when they leave, Love leaves. The other person was never in command
of your experience. You were—all the ups and downs and beauty of the
Love you experienced. The other person's presence in your life most
likely was a brilliant catalyst for your opening to Love, but you received
that dimension of infinite Love and welcomed it in. You allowed it to
move you and open you to the radiance of Love's eternal gift. Do you
really want to give the power of Love that is yours to another who does
not want to cocreate from the space of Love?

**We never need to fall victim to the emotion
of abandonment, for it is only a signal of our
separation from infinite Love.**

Relationship breaks can be filled with devastating feelings. We feel
our whole self, and especially our heart, bleed, scream, kick and yell.
We feel it collapse with a sense of abandonment, rejection and betrayal.
We may vow to never open our heart again to another. If we merely
stop at this level of experience, we are not claiming our experience
of Love, joy, peace and the beauty of our creation. We created the
whole experience. Why are we so quick to throw it away and separate
from it, just because another doesn't love and respect our creation of
Love?

We have the right to hold the sacred qualities of Love we received, experienced and magnified within the vessel of our experience of human relationship.

In the midst of our pain we forget that our sacred heart has never disconnected from infinite Love. It was the bountiful connection we allowed of the experience of infinite Love engaged in our hearts and bodies that compelled us to share our gift of ourselves with another.

If we feel deep emotions of loss, abandonment, fear or anger, those are parts of us crying out to remain connected to the Love we have expanded into. These emotional aspects in us are asking us not to separate from Love just because of another's choices around Love. Remember, your human heart is holding these feelings of loss, not your sacred heart. Let yourself feel the cry, the longing of those parts of you wishing to stay in Love. Bring them into union with your sacred heart and feed them with connection to infinite Love. Do not abandon it this time, for your own sake.

The Beloved sees us flourishing in the magnificence of all Love and creation.

The sacred heart never disconnects but we need to train the human heart that is open to the experience of human existence to change its direction in relationship to Love.

Priscilla was a woman who was devastated that her relationship with Joseph completed. She came to me collapsed and energetically shriveled. Her heart was feeling shattered and destroyed. She could not understand why her generosity of heart and Spirit and self had failed her. How could Joseph leave her, when she knew she had given everything to the relationship?

In our work together, the key that helped Priscilla so potently was the reminder that she just needed to train her human heart to know Love after the relationship completed. During her time with Joseph she had unconsciously, and at a soul level, taught herself to know Love through her opening with him. She was continually giving her heart the message that Love was being known because of Joseph. So, when Joseph left, her heart and many aspects of herself connected to this heart trained to know Love because of Joseph felt the devastation of loss and abandonment. I reminded her that we have all done this because we were not taught in school, or by parents or mentors, how to be in our sacred heart and how to let our personal heart stay in alignment with sacred Love. And no one taught us that the heart needs training in matters of Spirit and infinite Love.

When we have another to share the depth of connection to Love, our heart needs to be taught to shift its orientation back to being fed by connection through the sacred heart to infinite Love. As Priscilla feels the sense of loss of Joseph, it allows her the opportunity for her heart to move from loss to longing to reunion as an anchor for knowing and sharing Love again. She can teach her heart that infinite Love is *always* present. And is not going away. It is her job to connect those parts of her that have forgotten what her true anchor is of her own absolute connection to Love. When she reclaims that abundance, she can walk through the transition and reorientation of her heart with grace and ease. This way she stays open to Love, which never left. She has created it before for herself very beautifully, which is why she drew Joseph into her life, so she can do it again. That way she doesn't have to guard or close down her heart and can actually increase the magnet of Love that she is because of her relationship, regardless of Joseph's actions.

She was so relieved not to have to wallow in failure or self-pity but to see this as an opportunity to increase her own abiding connection to infinite Love, and allow her naturally generous nature to flourish.

All who have shared in your Love will remain in union with you, soul to soul, if you choose. That union allows all that is true of soul connected Love to continually allow oneness to be known and built here. This oneness, due to soul connected Love, is the transformational field that establishes the unified field of creation on Earth for us all to share in.

The True Witness

We are drawn to the world of relationship not only for Love but to feel witnessed in our life. The only true witness and acknowledgment is universal acknowledgment. This witness always sees, knows and understands you. That divine witnessing, filled with Love and understanding, is naturally going on continually. Through your soul you are connected in essence to everything, everywhere, of creation. So every other aspect of creation knows you intimately and is witness to the constant birth of creation called you. The Beloved knows and Loves you beyond your greatest imaginings. This Beloved loves you more than you could ever know. It holds you sacred, so you never have to feel that place that asks, "What about me? Who is here to witness my life?"

In the eyes of the universe you are precious. You are a sacred prayer of life.

Soul Mate Connection

When you vibrate at the level of union with your soul, you have found your true soul mate, your Beloved. As your heart and the cells of your body experience the ecstasy of this fullness and return home to wholeness within yourself, you are indeed a magnet for an outer soul mate relationship. Know that not just one but many may reflect that quality of union and intimacy of heart and soul in cocreation with you, in fact.

As you reunite in heart and soul with the Beloved that you have always been, ecstasy will roll into your life. It cannot help itself. And that partner of your dreams will be continually present in your heart and soul. He or she will surely arrive at your doorstep. The universe wants the depth of your union with infinite Love to be fulfilled here. In truth, we are creating a world of soul-filled, Love-filled soul mate connections. This is how oneness is embodied. This is how our world unites.

The places within you that have been guarded from knowing this experience of Love as oneness must reunite with your soul, through your heart. Then you can know soul mate Love within you, and thus be able to create it with another. Let those parts that have mistrusted absolute connection, or that have held back the flow of the Love, be welcomed by Love's blessing. The miracle of soulful partnership in Love will naturally find the lighthouse of soul mate Love that you are.

Family Connection

Inherent in our connection to Spirit is an exquisite system of guidance within us, to be connected to a universal network of collective guidance. We did not set up our life purpose with our parents and immediate family to be our primary guidance system or lighthouse. We chose our parents and immediate family based on our soul strengths, weaknesses and purposes, but they were not designed to connect us to Spirit.

It was originally intended for parents to reflect God in the physical, consciously creating as Spirit and inspiring their children to embody Spirit as well. But the blueprint for planet Earth, with this piece included, did not stay on track.

What I have discovered in my many years of working with the soul level of our purpose for being here is that often we chose parents and family members based on some of our soul weaknesses, not always our strengths. Sometimes we had contracts still pending to work out, especially with our mothers and fathers. It did not leave much room for them to represent godparents to us. They were busy filling other roles for us that we chose. These roles weren't necessarily present to magnify cocreation from infinite Love. Consequently, we may feel a deep longing for home and family within us that never seems to be satisfied. Nor do we understand where it comes from and how to have the sense of fulfillment of connection to home that we inherently long for.

We were intended to have parents available to us who represented God in human expression for us as a mentoring relationship of wisdom and knowledge. They were gifted to us to teach us how to live as spiritual beings in a physical dimension for its expression, throughout our incarnation.

The good news about this setup we currently have in which parents don't seem to do an adequate job of representing God is that because we didn't see our parents as God-like we were less inclined to have them play God to us. We could not easily see them as being in charge of our life. If we did put them in the role of being God, we might easily slip away from allowing Source and infinite Love to be our true guiding light.

When we have put our mothers and fathers in the position of God to us, it certainly has caused its share of tribulations. This causes deeper chasms of separation, as we let those outside ourselves exclusively hold the essence of home, family and Love to us. This becomes a wound of separation that includes disappointment and feeling of loss of home. On the other hand, it catalyzes us to reunite with our universal heart and home and the family of Spirit in the field of all creation as our true home and source of family. Familial relationships can devastate us as much as intimate relationships when we expect them to provide a spiritual anchor and Love that they are not capable of.

In this scenario of family, as with all relationships, the only true relationship to be known is between you and universal you. Then you can clearly see all of your other relationships for what they truly do and don't provide. You are then free to choose relationships based on cocreation, not based on serving the need for emotionally based love, approval, a sense of belonging or a place to be taken care of.

Our true spiritual family is with us, as an extension of us, in the field of all creation. We know its presence from being open to participate in connecting Spirit and form as one within us.

4

Expanding Connection with Creation

The wiring for health, wealth and happiness was given to us when we came into existence. All we have to do is push the refresh button to activate the right programming. It is a choice. The degree of our outer success relates directly to the degree of our "successful" experience of union with Spirit.

The Beloved sees us fully realized and successful as abundant creators continually.

Success

Our success is directly related to our availability to embody Spirit. This is a very different perspective than what we usually equate with success and our ability to be and feel successful.

Usually, we seek success in terms of attaining a particular goal that we deem important. Our definition of success continues to change for us. Success could be related to money, intimate partnership, a home, a great career, being good at a sport or a skill. You name it, it could relate to a lifelong goal or a personal best for the day.

Let's take success to a deeper level. Notice that you feel good about yourself when you have been successful in the ways that have value to you. You feel good, not because you have merely accomplished a desired outcome, although that can be part of the equation. Deeper within you, you feel good because you feel that you are a creator. You are available to creation in the ways that you value. You have not just produced a product but engaged in certain qualities of Spirit that are important to you.

Did you make a large sum of money? Yes, and more importantly, because on your path to making money you created the qualities of Spirit that are valuable to you. Therefore, you did produce the money that those qualities of Spirit carry in relationship to money for you. Having more money could represent for you gaining more peace of mind, quality of life, power or security. You first created the longing for those qualities of experience, then connected to them within sufficient aspects of yourself that the money became a reflection of your inner dynamic of creation of those qualities of Spirit.

Take a moment to ask yourself, what are the qualities of Spirit that I wish to successfully create when I say I want more money? When you have that money, it is in fact a direct reflection of those qualities of Spirit living within you that you equated with having more money.

These qualities of Spirit are generated from the activation of our spiritual connection to those qualities of experience we choose to have. Those areas we wish to be successful in we are actually saying we wish to open up to, to bring greater life into, to bring the field of creation into. This means, primarily, that we wish to know spiritual connection in more abundant ways in our life. And we wish to bring more aspects of ourselves that have been held in separation into connection with these qualities of Spirit we value to expand our success in our world.

The more you love to create, the wealthier and more abundant you will feel. Thus, you will magnetize more abundance to you in the ways that are vital to you. As you increase your connection to the field of all creation, your love of creating will naturally increase. Your love of creating is directly proportional to your Love of, and connection to, the field of all creation.

Remember, your true wealth has always been with you and can

never be lost. You will know this sense of wealth in your life, at all levels, through the amount of connection you have to your soul and Spirit. Your soul is connected to everything, everywhere. That is the connection to universal wealth that is always present and available. When we are available to that wealth of creation, we not only feel wealthy, but know the deepest sense of success. We continually know success in being the natural creators that we are designed to be. We are successful in being one with All That Is, bringing all aspects of our self into connection and embodiment of that wealth.

> **As you expand your connection to the wealth inherent in your soul, the whole universe supports your success.**

The Abundance of Expansion

As spiritual beings living through the magic of physical existence, it is our nature to explore and create, and thus expand in our capacity as a vessel to accommodate the larger universal symphony we are a part of.

It is the very nature of creation to want to expand in our life experience continually. If we are not creating, which requires life force connection, we are contracting. So, in order to fulfill our deepest urge, which is to create, our spiritual connection must be in motion. When our spiritual connection is in motion, life force is alive and well in us and creation brings forth expansion and abundance.

To expand in life we are giving ourselves permission to freely explore and experience all that we choose to create and enjoy. We say we want to know abundance in all ways. We are really saying that we want to engage as fully as possible in life.

Life itself optimizes abundance.

We certainly see this clearly in the magnificent palette of nature. Abundance is a quality of experience birthed from our connection to the field of creation, which is Spirit's universal palette. Abundance is divinity and its natural scope of limitless possibilities given expression at this level of creation. So, to know abundance, which is a quality of Spirit first and foremost in our inner sanctum as well as our outer world endeavors, we must first be connected to the spiritual dimension abundance heralds from.

Hourglass of Life

In order to expand in our outer creative life, we must first expand in our connection to Spirit and the field of all of creation that fuels our life. This is called the hourglass theory for life. We can't expand in the "lower" physical dimensions without first expanding our resources "above" to feed our outer expansion. Thus, I use the hourglass image. It is natural to want to experience a vast array of life experience and a greater quality of life. But to do so successfully our expanded connection to infinite life moving through us is required. As our capacity to engage with Spirit increases, so does the joy and fulfillment factor in our life. Whether this fulfillment speaks to us through the desire for a greater quality of life known financially, through our health, our capacity to know Love, or home and family, we are always saying that we want to know more of Spirit's wealth pouring through us—the wellspring for abundance and expansion.

To declare that we want more abundance and expansion, or freedom or power or Love, we must not only be willing to be open to a more expanded, abundant connection to the flow of Spirit through us, but to welcome more of ourselves to participate in our desired outcome. To create in larger ways, more of us must be unlocked from old, separated patterns, to participate in our larger playground. If we are a house divided, and only a small part of us is accessing the wealth of creation, our ability to expand is also hindered. When we allow those parts of us that are holding back to know infinite abundance, then we will truly create a more open, welcoming, expanded vessel for Spirit's infusion.

We may invite Spirit, but remember those aspects of you that have been held in separation have made you feel anything but abundant. They will start speaking up. They will let you know they are being held out of Spirit's abundance coming through you. So they will let you know what they need so they can assist you to be all you wish to be. It is natural for them to want to be with you to create your expanded expression. Remember, these parts have not trusted the Spirit's influence, so it is vital to create space for them in your sacred heart's trustworthy connection to All That Is.

When an aspect of separation expands in its expression in you, expand your connection to Spirit to an even larger degree than the cry of this hungry part.

As we bring those aspects out of separation into the field of absolute connection within us, we will have the capacity we need to draw in the abundance we desire. Your abundant expansion "above" and "below" will guarantee the increasing experience of abundance and expansion you desire in your life.

For years, my feeling of inner and outer success and abundance has increased in direct proportion to my connection to my spiritual resources. Our connection to our spiritual resources is designed to have an immediate impact on our lives in the here and now. That is the design for life.

There have been endless times that I have worked with clients to help them get connected to their spiritual resources for whatever it is they are longing to experience here, and each time their hearts were first filled with Spirit's support, blessing and backing of power in relationship to their longing, the physical creation of that longing came easily, on the wings of that expansion spiritually within them.*

---

*My book *Soul Radiance, Bring Your Soul Riches to Life* speaks to this very fully, and the book has twenty examples of sessions that punctuate the vital hourglass image for the way life truly works.

Land Mines in the Field

As you expand in your connection to infinite Love, as you expand in your capacity to give Spirit expression through your life, you may find that you run into obstacles in the field of your creation.

These land mines are none other than potholes, pitfalls of fear and resistance living within you, created most often in the name of such dynamics as protection from harm, safety mechanisms or walls to keep out unwanted experiences. As we grow and expand in our connection, those patterns put in place by us for safety and protection no longer serve us. They may even feel confining or imprisoning.

But now you are wanting to expand the creative influence of Spirit in your life. So it is natural that these prior protection mechanisms that once served you well no longer do. Now you fondly see them as land mines—factors in the way of your success. Don't forget, before you feel frustrated about the fact that they have cropped up, that you created them in the first place. With necessary understanding and self-compassion, you can see these "enemies" for what they are. You can invite these pitfalls and land mines to now be embraced by Spirit and your infinite connection to Love and let these aspects of you lay down their weapons—which you gave them—and become a part of the expanded field of creation you are now wanting to engage in.

Often the existence of the power of Love moving through you will cause preexisting factions to fly apart as though old patterns are being broken up, melted, dissipated or dissolved. As long as we let Love continue to expand through these old patterns, they will integrate nicely. If we get caught in judging or trying to move away from these patterns that we no longer are choosing to engage in, we take them back in again. When old patterns show up while we are enriching our spiritual wealth of connection, remember they are looking for a place to land within our abundance of connection. Let Love hold a space for the transformation of these land mines and they will willingly orient to the spiritual home you are providing.

These land mines may have previously been seen as factors beyond our control, or sabotaging mechanisms trying to stop us in our tracks or detour our progress. We even might have said that it was life getting in the way. It is not life getting in the way, but the old patterns of separation we created now holding us back. These challenges, sabotages and roadblocks, as we see them, often seem to be beyond our control and we may feel as though we have fallen into a state of justified victimhood. Often we can feel paralyzed by the perceived power we are giving these inner voices or feelings within us that feel so real and convincing.

There we are in an expanded state of consciousness filled with hope, lightness of being and strength of purpose. It's as if a dust ball comes into our view in contrast to that place of light in us, and we begin to put our attention on it and it starts to grow in importance. It can be felt as a wall, restriction, challenge or impossibility. We can either follow that dust ball of thought or feeling, creating it as our new perspective, or we can reel ourselves back to our previously valued space of connection in Love. It is always a choice.

Duane was wanting to move away from accounting and into his passion for the environment and helping with the Green movement. After our session he felt a deep sense of knowing of his passionate single focus for his new career and its development. He had a clear vision of his direction and how to take the necessary steps to open the next doors to engage his vision and perspective. A week later he called me filled with abdominal pain and a feeling that one of the doors that he felt was most essential to open might not be opening.

I reminded him that these roadblocks were the inner land mines showing up in his new creative field. These land mines represented those aspects of himself, held in separation, that were afraid to step into doing what he Loved for fear the world would not receive him. I taught him the reunion exercises you will learn in the last chapter of the book. He incorporated those fearful parts he had hired to protect him from potential harm. They were now needed to propel him the distance and he lit up like a beacon.

He had no problem creating his dream and taking it into the world now. The addition of these aspects of himself were now sources of power, full for his vision, and giving him the necessary sense of wholeness and courage to see it come to fruition.

When we choose to reunite with the perspective of connection that is always held in our sacred heart and soul, then we can begin to see these perceived roadblocks as parts of ourselves calling out to return and join us in being an expression of connection to oneness again. What we have seen or felt as obstructions are simply aspects of ourselves not yet aligned with the flow of creation that emerge through us when we are in the flow of connected presence.

Having a word to name these obstructions helps to reframe them in the moment. When you see or sense a land mine and instantly identify it, it changes your view of it. It goes from being seen as an obstacle or sabotage mechanism to an objective piece of information to deal with creatively. You might simply say, ah, that is one of those land mines in the new field I am creating for my greater success and abundance. You will notice this thought, pain or feeling that stems from a fragmented part of you showing up as a contrast to the new experience you have been having. This reframe from obstacle or limitation to land mine diffuses the power the thought or feeling has over you. You can now see it as a part of you that is outside of the new space you are generating of greater Love, freedom or expansion.

For instance, if you open your heart to love someone more than you ever have before, you might run into an aspect like a guardedness or safety feature to make sure you don't get hurt in matters of Love. Now that feature is asking you to be guarded or closed, or keep a distance from the person you are opening to. This land mine that you planted to keep you from getting hurt is actually hurting you more by pushing away the person you love.

Remember that our connection to infinite Love is the true security we need to be connected to and surrounded by to assure us that our experiences of Love with others are not filled with pain and rejection.

If you are afraid of failing due to a prior experience you saw as failure, there may be an aspect you hired to keep you small and not too powerful so you would not fail. Currently you might be passionate about a new career or creative endeavor that really makes your heart sing, but you run into this part you hired to keep you small. In this scenario the land mine of being small is truly holding you back and not so welcome to you now.

Just as a real physical land mine is buried deep in the soil, we bury our inner land mines so deeply that we may forget what we decided was necessary for our survival. When we run into it, we have forgotten that we created it and put it away in the first place, so we might have a tendency to blame the external world or our idea of God for its existence and placement.

We are responsible for the land mine's placement within us. As we have the integrity to own this part of us that feels like a detriment or obstruction, the land mine can no longer be seen as a deterrent but a wonderful part of us wanting direction out of its disconnected place of protection or comfort. It can now be seen and felt as a loving companion to our expansion, success and wholeness as we offer it a hand to reunite with us in our wholeness.

This shift of perspective makes us responsible for any negative spin on our world and our self. There is nothing out there trying to harm or destroy us. How refreshing to realize that we can always claim the place of connection and be in command of our life. Then we truly can be in service in this world by serving those parts of us in separation. We are a lighthouse from which we shine upon the wholeness of our human dimension so that it may come home.

Chasms of Separation as Land Mines

For many who see themselves as dedicated to bringing Spirit into their lives, there still appears to be a chasm between their love for Spirit as a guiding light in their lives, and their ability to live, on a daily basis, from these higher realms that inhabit their meditations and quiet moments. This chasm often shows up most vividly as a discrepancy between heightened times of a sense of oneness and unity, and the ability to walk through the challenges that show up on our journey through this life on Earth.

How do we bridge this chasm so that our outer life is a direct reflection of our spiritual vision and purpose? How do we bring every aspect of our human expression into union with our spiritual vision and purpose so that we can live fully from the dimension of infinite Love, creating from the universal field of all creation? How do we live as the spiritual being that we are, piloting the ship of life that brings our mission for being here into fulfillment, and to know that we and the magnificence of Spirit, through our soul and heart, are cocreating our map of life?

The Creation of the Chasm of Separation

The following scenario may sound familiar. There you are feeling peacefully and joyfully connected, buoyantly alive in the moment. Then a thought, person or situation comes into your consciousness and brings into focus a strong feeling that initially you are not fond of. Feelings often arise, like ocean waves, in response to your spiritual emergence. They take you right off course, like a ship pulled by a current to a place it never intended to go. It's like you are not the captain of your ship anymore. This feeling that is pulling you off course, out of peace and connection, seems to be in charge. Where did that union go? How could it so suddenly dissolve? How could a feeling have so much strength so instantly?

Let's take a moment to relax the defenses against this feeling that has emerged. Let's try to see it, not as the enemy, but a part of you that has been attracted by the beautifully rich spiritual moment you were experiencing. This aspect of you has appeared with the sole intent to experience the same connection you were radiantly extending.

Your world and the larger world, in essence, are one and the same. There is no separation. Whatever you hold inside you naturally radiates to the whole world. Your divine self and every aspect of you is a macrocosm of the whole world.

The Makeup of the Chasm

The fact is, Spirit permeates every aspect of creation. It permeates all we create. Even our emotions are an aspect of our creation. We have created them to keep us from being hurt, to protect us, to make us feel a sense of power in a moment of helplessness. Whatever the reason, we invited them in at some point to provide us with an answer to a perceived need. This may be a survival-based need or fear-based need.

When we expand spiritually into those parts of us that have carried fear, powerlessness or a sense of being unloved, they feel the safety of an expanded homecoming. They are choosing to come unlocked from the grip of fear and separation and be at home in the field of Spiritual connection you are creating.

As you deepen your connection spiritually and bring it through your heart into your experience, your world and the larger world is transformed. What has been held outside of that spiritual connection in you is magnetically drawn to that deepening of home base in you. So, as you increasingly bring Spirit into your experience, the world of emotion responds. It is longing to belong to the larger resource inherent in being part of Spirit's home base. It was not designed to be outside of Spirit's expression.

These land mines in your creative field, which have a tendency to stop our forward movement, are parts of us that we have previously placed in a role of protection to keep us from being too powerful, open, Love-filled or vulnerable to Spirit, lest we get hurt. They were placed on a false premise that if we are powerful or generous "bad" things happen. Now we are deliberately choosing to be more aligned with the power of Spirit and the potency of Love. Our protective emotions have become barriers to Love and spiritual power and really want a different job description other than holding fear, smallness and protection against imagined danger. They want to contribute to the magnification of Spirit through us.

As we bring our emotional realm into alignment with our Spirit, the emotions transform into sacred feeling sensations of Spirit. Feelings are our means to give Spirit expression. Our feelings express the depth and breadth of creation we choose to allow to move through us.

Like the land mines we created, the emotionally charged parts of ourselves appear in response to our expansion of connection. Now we are allowing them to play a whole new part in our longing for spiritual fulfillment. These parts want to have relationship within us, to wholeness not separation.

The truth is that any emotional land mine that reveals itself is asking to be loosed from the chains of its prior role of preventing you from knowing greater life-filled expression. If we simply reject, discard, resist or ignore this aspect of ourselves, we are simply saying no to or dampening our spiritual fulfillment. We are declaring that we are choosing to allow this aspect of us that we previously created in a moment of separation to remain separate and disconnected from the spirit that is alive and moving in us. We are saying that we have no place in our spiritual field of connection, so vital to us, for this part longing to know sacred reunion. It is so refreshing to reframe how we see this aspect of us.

We can now see this emotion as a beloved part of us trying to find its way home.

This aspect has been merely attempting to move, an expression of fear, sadness or helplessness, trying to find its way home again in the context of Spirit—your Spirit. There is nothing wrong with feelings known within the context of our spiritual expression. Feelings are part of our human capacity for giving our Spirit expression in life. However, emotions running rampant in separation from our purpose and our true spiritual passion only create a larger chasm inside between your sacred spiritual connection and its manifestation in your life.

If you ignore the emotion that arises in you, you are in essence ignoring not only an aspect of you, but an aspect of humanity that is represented by this emotion. Human beings want to be of service, but when you reject or deny a part of the human dimension caught in separation, you deny spiritual connection in a much larger context than just your emotional realm. It is all intertwined.

Consider what it means to be spiritually fulfilled. It would be reflected as a happy, healthy state of being in body, mind and heart. This includes feeling expression of life through body, mind and heart.

One client I worked with was not happy with his boss but felt he had to keep his job because the money was good, and at his age he wasn't sure of any alternative routes for employment.

In our session together, I guided him to connect with authentic power moving within him that he had lost touch with. As a result, he felt a greater sense of assurance that he could step beyond his comfort zone and explore new possibilities for work that would allow him to build strength of self and bring this newfound gift to others. As we were speaking about new avenues for his exploration, he felt a deep sense of fear arise in him about changing jobs and disappointing his boss.

This was a great example of a land mine revealing itself. There he was, back in reunion with his authentic power, and his fear arose. He could have been taken over by the fear and, as he reported to me in that moment, that sense of fear could stop him in his tracks and he would likely retreat back to his current job and feelings of helplessness.

I explained to him that this fear was a land mine in his new field of holding authentic, creative power. It was a part of him that he had created previously to keep himself safe, which also meant small and powerless. His authentic power was now "speaking up" to say it was ready to come out from hiding and join with him in bringing forth his creative power. It would be not only helpful, but necessary for him to tap and use this authentic power to move out of helplessness and find a more suitable job and boss.

As he allowed the land mine to merge into union with his authentic power, his fear dissolved and he felt lighter and more assured in moving forward.

Spiritual fulfillment in large measure relates to having every aspect of yourself connected, happy, healthy and whole. It means that we feel alive and engaged in life. The definition of wholeness and how it looks and feels for each of us individually keeps expanding as we explore what it is to be spiritual beings in the human dimension.

So it behooves us, if we are interested in being healthy, happy and whole spiritually, to include all our experience of body, mind and heart in this wholeness. Including every aspect of ourselves, emotional patterns as well, in our spiritual expression is paramount.

To see that emotions are merely parts of us longing to come home to be part of our expanded spiritual fulfillment is key. This puts a whole new twist on how to be a spiritual being in a human body. It makes bringing our spiritual vision into our daily life much more doable. Every challenge can be seen as a spiritual experience, not as a life lesson but as a continual opportunity for spiritual union and homecoming for every aspect of us, and thus every aspect of humanity. They are inextricably connected.

What I have called land mines in our field are what I used to see as the self-sabotaging mechanisms that appear whenever we expand our creative influence into our world. When we step onto a bigger playing field, make a decision that is related to playing bigger, or move out of a preestablished comfort zone, we often encounter these land mines. They may feel like sabotaging mechanisms to detain our longings from being realized. They come as fears, doubts, resistances, walls or problems. Often our first impulse has been to pin or blame these feelings on others, as though they created the perceived problem. We have also seen these land mines as negative, disruptive, even evil, influences from outside of us. These attitudes are nothing more than claiming victim to powers beyond our control.

The truth is that the land mines in our creative field are a natural consequence of our expansion and emergence. When we step into the greater abundance of ourselves, the land mines in this new field of our creation appear as aspects of us that have been held in separation and now wish to be part of the expanded field we are generating. These bumps that show up as contradictory emotions and physical discomforts are now coming to the surface to be part of our newness and greater embodiment of Spirit. These parts of us want to assist us in our expansion, in fact, not try to take away from our emergence as it may initially look on the surface.

As you create new levels of connection and soulful embodiment, welcome these incongruent aspects. Allow your creative field to be as powerful and bright as you can bear.

Protection: The Myth

Our need to feel protected and safe within ourselves, and as we move into the world, has increasing relevance in our thoughts. This need for protection shows itself to many who are concerned that their light and spiritual resources need protecting from harmful energies they believe are lurking in the unknown.

At the level of national security, safety and protection has become an increasingly visible part of our daily lives, from antibacterial soap dispensers in airports to massive military and security agencies put in place to guard and secure what is important to our nation and to the world.

We have told ourselves that if we increase the amount of protection we use, we will surely feel safer, whether it is energetic forms of protection through mantras or rituals, or tightened security measures in public places.

Many have for years thought that protection is an essential ingredient to conscious, spiritual health and well-being. It made perfect sense to need protection as a spiritually minded person in a crazy, dog-eat-dog world. Feeling protected meant that they could walk out of their door after a delicious meditation without the sense that it would dissolve in a moment, washed away by "bad vibes" out there. Many solidly believed this. We had our energetic protection plans, shields, energies, and soon that would take care of everything when bad things happened.

Invisible Enemies: The Myth

I often hear people speak of their vigilance to call in protection, ask for protection, and even pray for protection.

I honor our desire to keep what we value safe and intact. I honor our vigilance to keep what has meaning for us held as sacred and respected.

There is a hole in the well-meaning reason we have for protection. More often than not, when we ask for protection it comes from a place of fear. We want protection to keep us from the harm of that which has power, influence or impact on what we value. If we want protection *from* something we are saying we are afraid of it. We imagine the potential power that "something" has over us to threaten our ability to keep what we respect and hold sacred. What we hold valuable could be our physical or emotional well-being or the well-being of another. It could even extend to the health of our nation or the world.

Sometimes we might say that we want our travels to be safe and protected. Protected from what? Or we want our country to be safe and protected. Protected from what or whom? Saying this is declaring, albeit subconsciously, that there is an invisible enemy out there that has the right or power, in our subconscious, to take away what we value, or to harm or destroy it.

The invisible enemy stems from the ideas, feelings or beliefs we hold that a force larger than what we see and feel ourselves to be, can and wants to hurt us. These beliefs may have the reinforcement of soul memory, past life links or childhood scenarios. They have weight in our DNA and the collective DNA we have created.

The truth is that as long as we continue to support these feelings and beliefs it will keep this invisible enemy alive in our minds and emotional cells. It will keep us in a continual victim stance in the world and in ourselves. This reinforces in us the need to keep protection around, which develops into a barrier, wall or defensive stance. The protection becomes further solidified as a statement for the existence of power that seems greater than us. It reduces us to living a survival-focused existence. From there, we will never be including our connection to true spiritual power in our life.

I believe that the increase in sleep disorders and anxiety in our population comes largely from these unknown but prevalent feelings running us unconsciously. They say we are helpless to this power we can't control or contain in life. We are on the defensive energetically, once again bringing to the fore this idea of protection as essential to our health. This use of protection as a device to ward off what we see as harmful keeps us in a vice of powerlessness so we are not able to access our authentic source of universal power.

There is no shortage of people who misuse power due to their own insecurities, fears and lack of connection to their soul strengths. Their weaknesses and separation from Spirit pulls them to be devious and destructive. Their lack of value in life pulls them to take life force from others. Those invisible enemies do not need to be feared, for they are powerless in the face of true power. They feed off other's weaknesses, not their strengths. This translates into our lives as disturbances and disruptions that are attracted to us due to our fear of these perceived powers.

When we are in the place of true connection to our divine resources of Love, power and peace, we know that all is well. As we embody our natural divinity we hold a place of authentic assurance. This connected stance does not attract the behavior born of the desperate needs of those people who try to harm or take advantage of others out of their own wounds of separation.

As long as we believe there is "something" out there that holds a power in our life greater than the power of our connection to Spirit, there will be. As long as we feel we need to protect ourselves from this so-called enemy, we are keeping ourselves in the game of survival and struggle for power.

Protection Not Working

It appeared the protection plans weren't working. So we commonly became more fearful of the world beyond our protective control. We would add walls and barriers in ourselves, justifying the essential need for them, even though the walls of protection most importantly walled off our connection to Love.

In the end, imagining we need spiritual protection does not seem to have brought any peace to our hearts and minds, nor has it helped to keep away things we deem to be harmful.

Protection may be designed to bring about a greater sense of safety and security, but I see fear levels in people going up exponentially, in parallel to the increase in protective measures. The general population is getting more aggressive and reactionary as a defensive response to fear, powerlessness and hopelessness.

What is wrong with a world that requires conscious, spiritually oriented people to constantly think of protecting ourselves? This is why I began realizing that protection is a myth. It does not appear to be giving us the sense of inner or outer security we are looking for.

Beyond Protection

We are here for more than to simply survive and manage our lives. We are here to be grand creators, aligned with the natural powers of universal creation pouring through our physical capacity to express vibrant life. If we are living from that connected, fully alive and powerful state, survival and safety are naturally given. The need for protection becomes a moot point. The need to consider these invisible enemies of our own making no longer uses our life force. Without the feeling that there is an invisible enemy there is no hypervigilance that robs the energy needed to fuel our ability to move forward as a creator in life.

There is no sense of danger; there is nothing that feels dangerous when you are embodying infinite Love.

Being Held by Spirit

Imagine for a moment that you are reunited with the power of all of creation. Imagine that you are held and supported by its largeness and grace. Imagine that you are feeling how every breath brings you into intimate communion with Spirit. In this moment of communion, do you need protection from anything? Do you sense any bad things lurking that dominate this majestic power you naturally hold and emanate? The answer is no when you are truly in this place.

Is that being naïve or unrealistic? No. You hold this eternal presence of Love in your cells with the force of All That Is. It does not need any fear-based protection to sustain it, for all of creation sustains it. You feel a sense of being in a place of true authentic security that is trustworthy and abundant. You are in the place where the light of the soul burns brightly in your heart and body, and you feel deeply held by the universal Spirit that is you.

You are beyond the place of hypervigilance and helplessness. You don't believe something can hurt you and, therefore it won't. Yes, you will have the challenges of separation knock on your door, but they cannot enter in. You inherently know what it is to be in the right place at the right time, not in the wrong place externally or internally where your weaknesses and beliefs of victimhood and powerlessness draw helpless power mongers to you to feed on illusions of separation.

When you are connected you know all is well and that is what you draw to you. The space of sacred union is an extremely freeing place to live from, in comparison to the space you have held yourself hostage in, of feeling fearful and in need of protection. That is a limiting place to live from, even though we imagine that protection will allow us to feel free. In fact, it keeps us from knowing the true aliveness we seek when we protect ourselves.

As you become connected, there is a whole new energy beyond protection that is present to call in to support, enhance and magnify your declaration that you live from the power of creation.

You can call forth an energy, a light, a presence that honors, holds sacred, respects and loves all that you value. You can call in that energy to be with you and around you all the time as a beloved partner in your life. That energy is rooted in all that you know and trust of Love and divinity. With it there continuously, you don't focus on harm, evil or helplessness to external forces.

Soul reunion allows you to feel the natural power of being in, and being with, the presence of Love. It dissolves the need for protection. It dissolves the myth of protection.

We can avail ourselves to being in aliveness, courage, strength, greatness, confidence and Love. As we live from our creative, powerful, playful and innocent connected selves, the energies of magnificent abundance come in to surround us. This allows our soul's song to be magnified. Its radiance and potency do not leave room for anything else to be present.

We naturally draw in all these qualities of Spirit as we expand our heart and soul connection to Spirit. This is how we create a world of peace that does not have to defend against the invisible enemies of our creation or concoct a system of protection and illusory safety.

We value Love as our sacred anchor for living—it holds the true safety we seek.

Part Two:

Soul Reunion

5

SOUL-LEVEL DISCONNECTION

For as long as you have existed as a soul you have been connected to eternal life.

You were born from the source of all creation and your divine umbilical cord to eternal life has remained intact.

Because you are an individualized aspect of all divinity you were allowed to travel here to pursue your dream of experiencing the richness of creation. Through a physical experience you can commune with the abundance of life in the animal, mineral and plant kingdoms and experience oneness with other souls in human bodies. This earthly dimension gives many faces to creation.

It is due to free choice, given to each soul, that separation has occurred. Along the way there were times when you as a soul made a choice to disregard your vital umbilical connection to eternal life. You chose to look outside of creation for a source of Love or power. You made these choices innocently, imagining that something outside of the realm of connection to divine source might give you something of value.

This choice might have been born out of a sense of overenthusiasm, or a pure overlooking of the factors involved in the new situation that you innocently gave your life force to. You gave your vital connection resources to a power outside yourself that you assumed was connected, but wasn't.

These soul-level choices take on a myriad of looks in our physical experience. A child taking candy from a stranger, a young person being lured into the hands of a family confidante, a teenager caught in an enticing drug-related scenario or the attractive but misguided pull of the captain of the football squad, are all examples of innocently giving our life force away in places that we discovered were not healthy. These results are born of not having a full understanding or maturity in a given situation because there is not enough experience to back up our choices.

In each situation you voluntarily moved out of being connected to God, to let some other force play God. In that moment, you created a weakness of disconnection and separation in yourself. Even if it was done with innocence, the consequence of separation still occurred. The soul is never left in full disconnection, but it may need a divine soul shop that does soul repairs for the parts that are disconnected.

This is the work I have engaged in with clients for over sixteen years. I embarked on this journey of the soul dimension because I knew that the only wound was the wound of separation. I wanted to help bring soul reunion to those who were hungry for it, in the places where their souls had developed what I call barnacles that prevented the light of the soul from shining forth. Like a cloud in front of the sun that casts a shadow, these barnacles cast a shadow of separation on various aspects of life expression. The impact of these barnacles is unique in everyone's life and unique in the way they limit future experiences.

All barnacles, struggles, pains and limitations in the physical, mental and emotional bodies are effects of soul-level damage.

Our Fall from Grace: A Choice

Infinite Love has never left. It is in every cell and every atom of our body. Love is in the blueprint we live by. It resides in our DNA. *We* separated from Love. *We* chose to separate from Love, over and over again. This is the ultimate truth and responsibility we must own in ourselves to reopen the door to reunion and wholeness.

In any area or facet of your life where you are not knowing deep satisfaction, joy, success, power and a sense that life is magnificent, you are playing out the illusion of separation. Love is not being allowed to permeate your existence. It is your time to say, "Enough! It's not working for me."

Owning this truth is a great freedom. It allows all those parts of you that have been out of divine union and became impotent and needy, impoverishing your sense of health and well-being, to now come forward to reunite and integrate. These parts can hold a whole new place within you, and can now proclaim their part in your fulfillment of purpose and abundant life expression.

Our weaknesses come from a division within ourselves. This feeling of weakness comes because much of us, or some of us, is not being fueled by Spirit, hence it is weakened and becomes increasingly lifeless.

Just as a flower or plant cannot live without light and water we cannot live without connection to divine light and the nourishment of water, symbolized by life force. It's that simple. A plant withers and dies without sunlight and water. Parts of us wither and atrophy without divine light and life.

This applies to every aspect of our human dimension: emotional weakness or overwhelm, mental instability or confusion, physical limitations, from having a cold to having cancer and heart disease. The only disease we suffer from is the wound, the impact of separation.

This separation is born in a moment of weakness, when we chose to step out of our alignment with our divine connection as our source for our life movement. We chose something outside ourselves to be our compass or lighthouse. We feel lost when we don't have our inner compass to Spirit. Our "lostness" draws us to continue to look outside ourselves for a compass or sense of direction. Our weakness draws us toward others with a similar weakness because we may be looking for someone to assist us who has a power that we believe we don't have.

It is vital for us to recognize that our lack or limitation will drive what is drawn to us.

This is the way the law of attraction works.

The collective development of lack of alignment with Spirit on Earth is what caused what we have called "the Fall" that is portrayed in most religions and myths. When we, individually, or as a collective, have let go of our connection to the eternal resource of Spirit, we are acting out of separation from it. This becomes a pattern of weakness, for the power of Spirit, the power of Love, is the only true power. In that moment of weakness, due to a choice to step outside of our natural source field of light, an aspect of us became weakened. When we feel weakened due to disconnection, our sense of powerlessness turns into a sense of helplessness. This is sure fuel for the sense of victimhood, which attracts the energy of people or situations that wish to prey on our weakened state. These are the people who take advantage of us. Then we launch into feeling betrayed, abandoned or rejected, as our powerlessness and helplessness take us to the place of feeling out on a limb. We feel even farther from our inner anchor to infinite Love.

The fact is that we are the ones who first betrayed, abandoned or rejected our source of light. This is essential for us to recognize. Then it is crucial for us to own it and take responsibility for our original "fall."

All these patterns we feel victim to, or are suffering from and feel helpless to change, stem from our original choices to separate. So it is vital for us to own our self-created patterns of separation as the first step in soul reunion. Recovery is easy when we are open and available to say for ourselves that the only wound stems from the act of separation that we chose.

These patterns of separation that occurred at a soul level translate into our life experience in a myriad of ways. It may look like we let others play some sort of God figure in our life, to make us feel better about ourselves. We might take care of other's needs in order to feel taken care of or loved, because we have disconnected from knowing and embodying infinite Love. This is another way we give our power to those outside ourselves when we are disconnected. There are many ways that we get caught off guard in our state of powerlessness by those looking to be the outside point of power for someone else.

Our connection with God is never broken at the level of the soul and sacred heart, no matter how far you have detached yourself from sacred life and bought in to separation. Because of free choice, our pursuit to move away from Spirit to have a different experience, even though we may not realize we are moving away from Spirit at the time, will create more separation. All those things which you have allowed to come between you and Spirit will begin to have power over you. That is why you begin feeling helpless and limited. You have lost command of that aspect of your life.

Being in command of your life is an ability you are born with. The you that can be in command is the you that holds supreme your relationship to Spirit.

When we don't feel in command of our life we have a tendency to create from a place of individual will. We develop it when we are not connected to the will of the sacred heart, or authentic self. We begin to create our own will to guide us. This encourages a focus of the ego, often fueled by fight or flight, composed of fear and defensiveness. All are quite understandable consequences from the state of powerlessness born of separation.

Negativity as Powerlessness

Our belief in evil boils down to our fear of a power outside our self that we have given the command of our life. It may even be a simple belief system that we are opposed to. Our repulsion of it keeps it in the position of power over us. Those who appear negative, disruptive or dark are merely operating out of the weakness of their individual will and wound of separation.

Evil or darkness has no power of its own. It exists whenever Love is denied. It's that simple.

Love is the source of all of creation. Disruption is the result of the choice not to participate in creation. Evil is not an illusion. It is a real behavioral consequence produced by the Love.

Assaults of evil, the effect of separation, have never disrupted Spirit. So-called evil exists when separation is chosen. These assaults only influence other areas of separation or weakness. Like attracts like. If we are in a state of weakness, we feel powerless, helpless or loveless and unconsciously will be looking for an outside source of power. Consequently, we attract an "evil force" looking to feed off our search for power. Whether it be a whole society, like the Germans who attracted Adolph Hitler to lead them after World War I, or an individual attracting a situation of date rape, or an audit by the Internal Revenue Service. False power, or negative behavior, is born of separation. Those with unconscious or soul-level patterns of powerlessness are attracted to it.

The greater the so-called evil force, the greater the pattern of separation being acted out. Separation creates a space of weakness and a place of not feeling in command of one's life. Then the game of finding the other people or sources to buy into one's need to regain power begins. If individual will is combined with powerlessness, then destruction, harm, taking advantage of others, acts of senseless "evil" become the means to feel powerful again.

From the place of separation there is no real power to be known. It takes a cooperation and agreement to keep alive the pattern of destruction born of the powerless state of separation. As we hold fear of these individuals or situations, trying to show they have some sort of power or influence, we create a community of "support" keeping alive these patterns of separation.

The sensationalism around the terrorists of this world is an excellent example. Yes, they exist. Yes, their actions are the result of full-blown separation. And all our attention on them gives them the illusion of power they need to keep surviving. They employ our collective wound of separation and the power we hold in our own "darkness" while we at the same time fail to see the power we give them. As our shadow elements of separation stay in shadow and are withheld from light, by our internal choices, these shadows subliminally run our life. They hold power in us. And so it is with these terrorists, our biggest enemies, as we perceive it. They reflect the terrorists in us, hijacking our lives. They are created in us because we let these parts of ourselves pull on our life force, robbing us of our ability to be expanded, rich, sacred conveyors of Love.

All we can do is embrace and reclaim those patterns of separation in ourselves that make us feel we are limited, incapable or undeserving of knowing life in all its glory. Even though we may have pockets of separation influencing our behavior, our life force does prevail. It is always a choice which stream we wish to focus our attention on, the stream of separation or the stream of connection.

Each time you claim that Love and universal Spirit is in command of your life, that reverberation moves into the world. When you opt for Spirit's guidance, you give it the greatest place of value within you. Anything less than that field of creation is simply washed away because you give it no more weight, in your heart. You declare in your actions that life prevails. As bullying is stopped in your world, either as the one being bullied or the one bullying, you have no more space for the power struggle that goes on through these larger terrorist patterns.

They deeply love and respect their state of separation and what they can do with it and how they can hold it over others who are holding the weakness of separation as well.

It is our mission to hold our sacred union and partnership with the Divine with such ferocity and passion that we simply watch the other patterns dissolve.

When we reunite with light, we carry a beacon within us of light and there is nothing that our light cannot "see" or perceive. When light is present there is no sense of harm lurking. Even when we feel someone operating in separation, our inner barometer of light allows us to naturally feel safe.

Our only job is to be connected, and embody Love. Does this seem unrealistic in the face of the atrocities that we know are happening in the world today? From the perspective of connection to Love we are actually able to see clearly what contains light and what doesn't, without judging it or labeling it bad or harmful. The heart stays open and we can continue to expand as radiant life even when evidence of separation is around us. We do not give it power because we are not in a mode of separation and fear, and thus in the place of giving our power to anything outside ourselves.

Whatever moment or experience or situation you have cut off from the gift of Spirit, that moment for potential connection is essentially condemned in your heart. When you cut off Spirit you are judging it and saying it is not of value to you in that situation. That is the ultimate judgment. That is the ultimate act of destruction—to deliberately use judgment to declare that the power of Spirit has no place in you, and you choose to move in life without it. You are destroying life, for yourself in this instance.

Our Inherent Guidance System

From the beginning of time we have had a built-in sensory perception system. Long ago it was used for the basic needs of selecting foods and medicine, determining who was friend and who was foe. Animals have held onto this perception, so they inherently know what is true and Love-filled and what is not. A bird deciphers the difference between a poisonous seed and a seed that is nourishing. Our perceptive sense of what is operated by light and what is not is very practical, not just mystical. It was given to us so that we might navigate all facets of our physical life with grace and ease.

Incarnation

Physical incarnation is always voluntary. Your soul has chosen to come here to experience physical life. Most of us brought soul barnacles with us when we came here for this incarnation. Many developed those barnacles after arriving here.

Many people are aware that the patterns of separation that you are currently experiencing go deeper than childhood. And these patterns most likely feel as though they're getting deeper and more entrenched as you walk through life. They influence not just cellular memory but DNA.

This physical incarnation was not designed for separation, so that we might first forget and then remember. The thought feels exhausting. Why would Creator and eternal life create such a challenge? It was our inclination to participate in realms and experiences that were separate that created the forgetting. Our soul and sacred heart, our essence and essential nature, have never forgotten their origins and the Love that fuels all of creation.

When we delve into patterns of fear, separation, skewed perceptions, emotional taints and limitations, we see a choice was made over Love. The more these patterns of weakness and separation grow in us, the more we forget. Remember that the whole universe and every soul supports you in creating from the power of Love.

Specific Soul Patterns

When each of us was one and complete with all that is Love, we were given the gift to be a unique particle of creation known as ourselves. This was to be our soul's individual experience as light birthed into life.

Even though free choice was involved in this beautiful experience of individuation, many took on various mistranslations or misperceptions of their new state as a soul and have carried that wound ever since. These soul dynamics that I am describing are at the core of many of the deep issues we all seem to carry and play out in our lives.

Some have seen this new state of individuation as rejection by the oneness, the completeness, as though they were being kicked out of the nest of oneness. Others have taken on a feeling of being abandoned by Creator, as though they had to lose their heart and soul connection to be an individual soul aspect of Creator.

We were meant to be extensions of Creator, in oneness always, not individual aspects outside of Creator.

A number of souls were so enamored with the gift of individuation and the uniqueness of their presence that in their overzealousness they betrayed their supreme connection to Spirit that allowed them to *be* in the first place.

Some have carried a pattern of betrayal. When they individuated they took on their personal will and made choices from that place. When those choices did not please their personal will they felt betrayed by Love, as though divine Love got them in trouble in the first place and was not getting them out.

Soul-Level Betrayal of Love

I have met very few people who feel complete in their heart and soul in the experience of feeling deeply loved and wanted in this human dimension.

We came here with various patterns that left us feeling unloved and unwanted. Like Little Red Riding Hood, we were caught off guard by a wolf in sheep's clothing, so to speak. In that moment we bought into a false form of protection or caretaking dynamic of Love. In doing that we actually made the choice, in innocence as a young soul in relation to energies that were outside of infinite Love, to let go of an aspect of pure connection to infinite Love. It was a trade-off. Consequently, we have not been able to reestablish a heart filled with a sense of home, or a heart that felt it could receive and take in Love at the human level. In the majority of cases, this stems from a soul-level betrayal of connection to Love. The only way to feel loved and wanted in life is to be connected to infinite Love and the universal oneness that can be seen and felt as connection to home and spiritual family that resides in infinite Love. The soul and sacred heart has continued to be held in infinite Love. Our universal family wants us to thrive and it sees us as its beloved extension into the human dimension. When we restore our connection in the places within us holding the wound of separation from infinite Love that leaves us feeling unloved and unwanted, magically we attract and develop connections here that magnify our sense of being a part of Love and wanted by Love. This is how the law of attraction works. When we hold absolute connection within us that will not betray infinite Love, we attract those who are inspired by our absolute connection that wish to cocreate in Love with us.

Holding Back Your Sacred Gifts

Another pattern of separation was formulated by souls at the time that they came into this Earth field. Imagine yourself as a soul outside of the gravitational field we are so familiar with. Let yourself sense how you might see from your soul dimension. As you approached this world you began to perceive the density of the gravitational field here. You sensed that it was very different here than the atmosphere you were currently "floating" in freely. You had been told by other souls how distinct this world is and that there were a large percentage of humans existing in a state of disconnection with Spirit. That was fine for you to grasp conceptually. You knew you had agreed to come with the purpose to help those in disconnection to reconnect with Spirit. Besides, the natural world here was exquisite, like no other place you had been, so you were excited to experience the wonder and beauty of this amazing world. You were opening to the experience of the six senses in the physical dimension as never before. The magic, the aliveness, the joy inherent in human life expression was a great pull to come here, even if many humans existed in separation. In that moment as a soul you were clear that your connection was real, and not in danger.

As you felt the reality of this density and impact of separation on those here, you began to put on the brakes and question why you were bringing your precious light and gifts here, to what seemed like a place that carried very little understanding of the kingdom of Spirit that you were holding and connected to. You couldn't imagine feeling honored, respected or supported by this human population steeped in their existence born to a large degree of separation. It didn't feel true to your heart to let your Spirit be tainted by this cloudy human behavior, nor did it feel wise to be sharing your wealth with those who had no room to appreciate your brilliance. It felt like casting pearls before swine.

So you made an executive decision within yourself to hold back in bringing your sacred, holy nature, or your radiance and joyfulness. Or you saw no reason to bring the supreme power of Love that you were one with. It might be destroyed, demolished or crucified. So you left your gifts at the doorstep, so to speak, and shifted your energy field somewhat to be more like the energy of this human population immersed in fear and separation. You did this with the distinct sensation that you would be "dumbing down" to be more like the majority here so you would feel accepted. Maybe you would even feel like you belonged. *Then* you could assist and serve and bring your wisdom and truth more easily and effectively.

You decided that it was somehow more important to have a place here than to stay connected to, and bring forward, your sacred gifts and soul purposes. It was even more important if that meant you were betraying your holy connection to Spirit to feel comfortable in the human world that was before you.

Does this scenario match your current life in any way? Do you feel like you don't belong? At the same time are you afraid to shine and be all that you are because you might be even more ostracized than you already feel? Do you feel like you have tremendous wealth to offer, but you can't seem to be able to find it or get hold of it? Are you aware that you have sold your soul to belong, or feel Loved and connected to people here, even though your interaction with them doesn't fulfill you in your heart and soul?

Maybe you are suffering from this soul-level syndrome of having left your gifts behind, so they would not be harmed. If that is the case, it is time to reunite with your soul's wealth and reclaim it. In that moment of choice to drop your abundant nature, the only one that truly suffered was you. If you had checked in with the universal council of creation guiding you in matters such as travel to a whole new world, you might have proceeded differently. You might have been reminded that the only reason for moving anywhere as a soul is to bring your universal gifts of connection to Love.

It doesn't matter what anyone else's choices are, even if it appears that the majority are choosing separation. Your purpose was and is to experience the joy of creation being given expression through the human dimension that planet Earth afforded you.

It is very natural to feel that it is ludicrous to come into a world that is not filled with Love and connection. But take note of the fact that it is even more ludicrous for any of us to leave our connection to Love behind, just because it isn't present here. We left behind the pure connection to Love and oneness to feel a part of this world. This world had abandoned Love and connection to a large degree, so we consequently were choosing to be part of a world that abandoned Love.

Now we might be able to see how we only harmed ourselves by making a choice outside of alignment with divine guidance. The resulting choice took us out of the arena of creation into existence in survival mode in varying ways. As we are now shining light on our previous behavior, we can see our faltering and how we are truly the ones to be held accountable at a soul dimension for any of our suffering. When we buy in to mere survival, we have separated from our light. We end up engaging in caretaking love instead of real, inspirational, divine Love. We were designed to bring the inspiration of what it is like to be so utterly plugged in, so that we are living examples of what it is to be in Love with life itself. So, when humans decide to move out of fear, we are shining with the choice that radiates the abundance of union with All That Is. Others then proclaim, "I want to *be* what that radiant person is, who feels in complete command of their life."

Our Right to Exist

When we look to others to give us our sense of meaning or to give us approval, we are denying our connection to Spirit as our purpose. We are denying the power of the universal family and home of Love to ignite our life. Whenever we seek permission from the external world simply to exist, we see the external world as keeping us down, not allowing us to exist. When we feel utterly surrounded by the natural gifts of infinite Love, we have no doubt of our value and strengths. How the world sees us does not matter, for we feel deeply seen by the beloved All That Is.

Love as Security

When you are ready to let go of the game of separation and rise to the level of connection to all that is abundant and life-giving, you will see and experience your relationship to this world very differently.

Imagine for a moment that you are reunited with the power of all creation. Imagine that you are held and supported by its largeness and grace. Imagine that you are feeling that your every breath brings you into intimate communion with Spirit. In this moment, do you need protection from anything? Do you sense any bad things lurking that hold sway over this majestic power you naturally hold and emanate? The answer is no, if you are truly in this place.

It that being naïve or unrealistic? No. As you hold this eternal presence of Love in your cells, the force of Spirit is truly with you. It does not need any fear-based protection to sustain it, because all creation sustains it. The universal power of Spirit sustains you in every cell. You feel in a place of true authentic security that is trustworthy and abundant. You feel the flame of the ignited soul burning brightly in your heart and body.

In this sacred place of communion you are beyond the disconnected place of feeling helpless. There is no sense of hypervigilance and fear that something can hurt you. The challenges of separation still knock on your door, but they cannot enter in. You inherently know what it is to be in the right place at the right time.

Love is the only true safety net.

Soul Depletion of Power

Another soul-dimensional pattern of separation pertains to depletion of power.

Once you were a magnificent, powerful soul. Your power came from your absolute connection to source and its power. You were traveling in this universe, heading with enthusiasm to planet Earth to show the human beings what true power is, and how to embody it, as you have. A group of souls approach you and you can feel that they feel a resonance with your power. They are awed by it. And they tell you that they are versed in earth-level power. They will teach you about that, if you agree to do an exchange of their earth-level power for your power.

How wonderful and convenient that they came right to you with this valuable information! You agreed so you would be up on how earth power works as you entered into the Earth field for the first time.

Perfect … seemingly. You forgot. *You* are holding the only true source of authentic power. What is this earth power, if it is different? You assumed it was an extension of the true source of power.

As you know now, the power that is used in the Earth that they wanted to teach you about is fear, greed, manipulation and the misuse of power over others. So learning these methods is not so productive after all. But there you were, stuck with this agreement to make this exchange. When you do so at a soul level it comes with you throughout your incarnations.

How does this look in life? In the most basic description, it shows up in real time as your inability to hold your power. You had agreed that when you came to Earth you would use the nature of earth power that these souls had said they would set you up to use. So now, whenever you choose to be your authentically powerful self, you lose your footing, you get taken advantage of, you fall into feelings of helplessness that you don't have the power and divine strength you need. You feel you have lost connection because you stood up to shine in your wholeness.

This may show up in little ways, or at pivotal points in your life, depending on the degree of your buy-in. Remember, these souls, these "power mongers," were operating from the place of separation, in need of authentic light power to keep them going. They can only feed off the life force of others if you make it available to them. In this case you happily gave it. It takes two to tango. Your mission to bring forth the power of oneness was betrayed by your choice to take on their game as your operating plan. You chose to take on their operating mode instead of holding sacred your connection to universal power.

In this situation and in the others I have described, we who have been influenced by any of these patterns that bring separation often lose trust in Spirit. The truth is, we don't trust our ability to stay connected to the fact that Spirit is working in our everyday life.

Trust Your Connection

The simplest, most effective way to regain that trust is to exercise your ability to be connected to the inherent power that you have been merged with and immersed in since the beginning of your existence. It is essential to gain a soul perspective and move beyond the limitations of separation into the field of all creation. The soul's engagement in the process of reunion is essential.

As individuations of Spirit we are always called to cocreate. That is how connection to oneness and wholeness dance in the universal arena of life.

By choice, we abandoned our connection to Spirit. We rejected Spirit's place in us. We betrayed creating from divine will in unison with our will as an act of cocreation.

These patterns hold soul-level duress. And they play themselves out through our ongoing patterns of trauma. This could show up as birth traumas or relationship traumas, every measure of pain that might be named abandonment, betrayal or rejection issues at the emotional, psychological level.

All these ramifications stem from the deepest wound of separation at a soul level. Abandonment or loss of connection to Spirit and Love in some part of us is at the root of every wound we hold or perceive, played out over and over again in our lives. Our soul life is always guided by the command of Spirit. It is our separation that creates a lack of life force in us that produces struggles and limitations. Soul level separation plays out through ongoing patterns of trauma in our lives. This includes all manner of birth traumas, relational difficulties and ability to function well in life at the physical and emotional levels.

For example, Claudia came into my office and immediately said, "I'm afraid. I don't want to look for a job." She felt claustrophobic, as though she had a straitjacket around her body.

I suggested that the fear was tied to aspects of herself that were afraid to change. The fact was they felt paralyzed to move forward; the fear and claustrophobia she was feeling was evidence of her pattern of separation. It was natural that this aspect of herself was afraid to move forward. It was caught in separation. It was crying out to be unlocked from its straitjacket, to help her on her campaign to find a new job.

I asked Claudia what this fearful part of her needed. What is the greatest gift you could offer this aspect of you at this time? "Love," she said. "Connection to divine Love." I had her use a simple image that represents real Love to her and breathe it into her heart, even if she was having trouble breathing.

She said the image was hard to trust. I reminded her that this was the fearful part speaking. I told her to let that aspect feel her sacred heart and its connection to Spirit, which we had previously explored. See that the fear and her sacred heart were two different dimensions. I had her start showing the fear the choice of connection to the sacred heart. I reminded her "Let the heart be the anchor of home base the fearful part is crying out to be connected to, so it can first know that divine Love is always present. Secondly, let the fear have a new place and be a part of your movement forward." We let her shattered part be held by Love. I reminded her that when her parts cried out, she could say from her sacred heart and soul space, that is always connected, "Love is here." As she brought that claustrophobic, fearful part to Love, it melted and transformed to a space of freedom. This freedom in Claudia had been "locked away" out of a sense of the need to be protected from harm. Freedom meant disaster somewhere in her. Now freedom, connected to the anchor of divine Love, opened a large door to explore a whole set of new possibilities she had not seen before.

6

Beyond Separation to the Ultimate Frontier

As a soul comes into the human dimension to give magnified expression of itself, these soul barnacles play out as disturbances in all realms: physical mental, and emotional.

Feelings versus Emotions

Humans were designed to be Spirit consciously experiencing creation into the physical dimension. There are infinite possibilities to give life conscious and radiant expression. We are not designed to emote. We are designed to experience the magnificence of life through the sense of being passionately alive and peacefully satisfied. We are designed to feel life through the six senses, not live in the reactionary realm in which emotions play.

For example, an actor knows that he is giving expression to a particular feeling state in any given moment. His ability to move in and out of various feeling experiences is what makes him a great actor. It may look like emotion, but for the actor it is an experience in the moment that he is actually detached from. His only desired outcome is to give authentic expression in the moment. He may bring experience, great depth and meaning to the feeling but he can step out of it easily. It's unlike our experience when we are in emotional reaction and we cannot let go of the anger or fear that has us in a vice. Emotion is just reaction to a given state we come upon.

Emotions have taken over in human experience because we have dwelled in separation, out of reach of feeling experience. Feeling experience is the true expression of creation.

There are common emotional states that we hold onto as victims in our state of separation. From this separation we feel fear, limitation and powerlessness. Aliveness, joy, buoyancy, ease, strength and flexibility are feeling experiences or qualities of Spirit; they are not emotions. These feelings are known when we are in union with Love and creation, giving Spirit expression.

Emotional discord and turmoil are the result of separation. Mental instability and physical pain also grow out of the state of disconnection we have chosen. All these states of discomfort, disease and instability are the cries of the emotional pain of separation. The body, mind and emotional realm in the state of separation voices its desire to be reconnected. Our emotional realm can be extremely useful to us if we can see it from this perspective.

Human emotions in and of themselves can be dangerous aspects of separation, but when they are connected to the expression of our Spirit, they become useful means to experience the endless facets of life experience we choose to engage in. For example, when we say we are feeling desperate we are in truth feeling a desperate lacking of connection to Sprit. When that emotion of desperation is offered the opportunity to be a part of our connection to Spirit, we can see it as a desperate cry for anchor that only the consistency of Spirit can bring.

All Discomfort is Born Out of Separation

Any unwanted sensation felt through the physical, mental or emotional realm is a signal to let us know that we are in the midst of a space of separation from Spirit. That aspect of us is calling, crying out and seeking assistance to be fed with connection to the life force it is missing.

We know this most graphically with physical pain or discomfort. The body lets us know where it hurts and how it wants assistance. The bottom line of all assistance required is life force. When we see how simple this is, it is much easier to work with healing any wound or discomfort at any level.

All wounds are wounds of separation. The ultimate cause for all maladies in any realm is the lack of life moving into that realm in any moment; holding separation from the all-embracing Love and infinite presence.

Allowing a Connected Place for Our Emotional Experience

We will always feel. It is part of the human experience. If we are living as our authentic self, there is a vast array of feelings to be known as a part of the abundance of human experience. Feelings that are connected to Spirit, such as joy, peace, abundance or harmony, will create wholeness, fulfillment, satisfaction and expansion in us.

Emotions are different than feeling expressions. The distinction is extremely useful to understand. Emotions are born out of lack of connection to Spirit. There is nothing wrong with human emotions. They just need to be connected to the expression of our Spirit so we can experience the endless facets of life experience we choose to engage in. For example, when we say we are feeling desperate we are behind that emotional need, feeling desperate because we are lacking what we need of connection to Spirit. When that emotion of desperation is offered the opportunity to be a part of our connection to Spirit, we can see it as a desperate cry for an anchor that only the consistency of Spirit can bring.

The cry might be, "I desperately need more money." It is a very real emotion being felt. It is a certain cry for help, assistance, support, answers and clarity of direction to know how to end the misery felt in the situation.

The emotion "I desperately need money," shows up. What is truly being said is, "I desperately need to get in touch with the resources that create the movement of money into my life. I desperately need to get reconnected to my resourcefulness, which is a quality of Spirit. I need to reunite with Spirit and the field of all creation in the arena of what money holds for me (abundance, quality of life, success.) That part of me that is emoting the sense of desperation around the lack of money is simply wanting to reconnect. When I get connected to that resource of creation, and know it to be a part of me, then creating ideas, motivation, and a sense of inherent wealth can open and birth all sorts of possibilities to produce the physical resource of inner wealth that money rightly symbolizes."

When you feel desperate because someone important to you does not understand what you need, it opens you to a deeper place of learning because you are not getting what *you* need. Is it really another person's job to heal your wounds of separation that *you* created? If you allow the part of you in need to be fed by Love moving through you, someone else will surely be able to assist you in magnifying that Love in you. When you are connected in your heart and soul to Spirit, you are given abundant resources in whatever way is true for you in that situation. You then cocreate generously from that place of fullness with others.

Does that mean when you are united with the beloved All That Is there would be no need for others in your life? Absolutely not. But their part in your life would not be to fill your desperate needs coming from your feeling of separation. They would be fully engaging with you in cocreating from wholeness.

Another example of an emotion that signifies separation is anger. Anger is an emotion we feel that is born out of the recognition that we feel powerless. When we are separate from our true inner power source, we will certainly feel powerless. We feel angry that we are disconnected and therefore separate from our authentic source of power. Authentic power comes from feeling connected to universal power in our body. The same quality of energy is used in delivering anger as in delivering power, just at very different octaves energetically. Anger is born of separation; authentic power is known from being connected to the universal power in our body.

It is not wise to try to deny our emotions. They are parts of us held in separation trying to find their way home to Spirit's hearth. Anger stems from feeling powerless. When we connect our anger to our home base we feel the power of creation replacing the powerlessness of not being able to tap into our true creative nature.

It is our job to open the door to that unfulfilled part of ourselves to know the fulfillment of being a creator again. This emotion of anger is, in essence, saying, "I don't want to exist in this place of powerlessness. I want to engage as a quality of Spirit." In this case that quality is power. It is moving from being an emotion of reaction to an expression of a quality of Spirit. We want this experience of wholeness for all aspects of us. That is the most loving act we can do for ourselves.

I read a beautiful true story of a woman who had just lost a brother she was deeply close to. She had every right, from a human perspective, to be grieving her loss at every turn.

Grief and sadness, as emotions in and of themselves, stem from the feeling of being disconnected from Love. Grief and sadness are known when we feel the absence of a particular experience of Love we have known. When someone dies, we are sad we won't be able to share various experiences of Love with them. When we feel sadness as an expression stemming from an experience of Love such as this, it is a feeling experience of Love,

The woman in the story took her emotion of grief and held it in her heart and transformed it to Love. When she saw the gut-wrenching pain in her parents' eyes, she said, "This is Love." When she received words of consolation from friends, she felt that as Love. When she was with her brother's wife and children throughout the process, she kept saying, "This is Love." When she felt her brother, she said, "This is Love." She chose to see it all through the eyes of Love. Is this denial? Or was it the gift she received from her brother that she chose to keep alive and well in her sacred heart, as she had known it in his presence in her life? "This is Love" is truly the statement of infinite Love, and it can be applied to any situation we are in.

Connection is Always Accessible

In any situation, no matter how unavoidable it feels, the lifeline to Spirit is always accessible. You can remember to reach for and hold onto that lifeline, and know its bounty in every aspect of you. Your eternal self is helping you by presenting the perfect situations so that the parts you abandoned can come forth and be reconnected to your eternal self and the embrace of life. The gold in that wound is waiting and ready to be mined.

You are learning to overcome the tendency to deny the aspect of you that is crying out to know connection with your beloved self. Each time part of you that had been trapped in separation is brought back to its place within the unified field of your soul's expression, you will know a greater sense of yourself as Love, power, freedom and aliveness. To embody all that we are is the place we all long for. It is our divine homecoming.

Unwanted emotions or feeling sensations are the unacceptable parts of us calling for Love and illumination. Our emotional state tells us very specifically where the patterns of separation are. Each aspect of our expression that has been imprisoned in the state of separation, either as an ancient pattern of separation at a soul level or a current pattern of separation, longs to be reunited with Spirit through our sacred heart and soul.

They become attention grabbers, letting us know that they are ready and wish to be unlocked from being held captive, to exist with light within us.

As we awaken to this beautiful process of reclaiming these impotent or self-destructive aspects, these parts take on new roles or jobs within us to assist us in our path and purpose in wholeness.

It behooves us to see our pain and suffering in this light, so that we can shine light upon and illuminate these lost aspects.

We Alone are Responsible for Our Reunion

It is our job to hold the soul perspective of connection for those parts of us that are simply lost in the impact of disconnection, so that we give true soul nourishment where the need arises in us. So often when we are hurting we wish for others to be our resource to fill our needs and take us out of our pain. Momentarily, we may feel that others give us what we think we need, but it is only a temporary bandage for our discomfort, and the condition and pain of separation will return. The hunger, the cry for the soul nourishment that comes from our uniquely abundant connection to infinite Love is ours to fulfill, so that we are whole within ourselves. This is truly what we long for.

We seem to hold in our cellular memory this deep-seated propensity to look outside ourselves for our needs. This is what got us in trouble in the first place. It would be a different world if everyone got reconnected to the qualities of Spirit they are longing for, rather than expect others to fill up their tank.

What we are actually seeking when we ask others to feed us, if we look more closely from our heart and soul, is connection to the qualities of Spirit. Those qualities of Spirit born from our reunion to the field of all creation are always available to us.

It is also more efficient and productive to go to our inner source of connection to Spirit to fill the aspects of us caught in separation. We are the ones who created the pattern of separation, so our heart and soul know exactly what is needed to reunite with what has been lost. We chose the path away from Spirit, so the most direct route to recovery and fulfillment is through making the choice to rekindle our connection to Spirit.

If we continue to go outside ourselves to fill those unmet needs of our own making, we most often will feel ever more helpless, powerless and incapable to regaining what we abandoned in the first place. This relates to Love, success, wealth and health of body, mind and Spirit.

Remember these qualities of Spirit we are longing for were once known in our soul and sacred heart, so they are easily retrievable. We would not long for something if we did not, at some level, believe it was possible to attain. We only long for those experiences that our soul wants us to have and knows are possible to have. We have tasted the essence of them before and have simply lost track of them in our outer life circumstances.*

The soul is designed to be connected to everything in the field of creation. When you connect those aspects of you that have been struggling in separation to your Soul, infinite possibilities open for your prosperity. The universe most certainly teams up with your soul to deliver what has been felt to be lacking for you.

Receiving Spirit's Wealth

If you ever felt you didn't know how to connect to your soul's wealth and infinite Love, remember Spirit is always showering you with the gift of abundant life. We have, in various aspects of our life experience, shut off these gifts from coming through. We did this through the choices we made to let something outside ourselves be in command. The consequence is the pattern of separation we subsequently generated. Understanding this, we can now return those parts to be available to Spirit's wealth again.

---

* I speak much more on this topic in my book *Soul Radiance, Bring Your Soul Riches to Life*.

You might also have felt that you prayed for, opened yourself up to or surrendered to infinite Love and Spirit's guidance. Then you felt as though nothing happened. You felt your longing was left unanswered. You felt your heart crying for a drop of spiritual nourishment.

To receive Spirit's wealth, the aspect within us that has become dry and hard because it is being held in separation must make itself available to the outpouring of Spirit again. Reuniting with spiritual nourishment is essential as the first step. The heart must be softened and tenderized to be available again.

As you open the places within you where separation has caused hardness, the opening draws in the fullness of Love and connection.

Imagine that every aspect of you that has known separation can be restored. Imagine that this restoration is possible because of your connection to the true nourishment these parts desire and deserve. It is simply a matter of connecting those parts within you, in separation, to unite with Spirit through their connection first to your inner home base—for those parts and for Spirit.

Home Base

It is natural to want to be whole and happy. It is an inherent longing within us continually, and there are a variety of ways to fulfill it, such as having more money, children or relationships, therapy or spiritual growth work, using alcohol, drugs or stimulants. When we are deeply honest we can recognize that at the core of all our desires is the longing to know happiness and wholeness. These are qualities of Spirit that we crave. So doesn't it make sense that the simplest way to know these qualities is through direct connection to the source of them? Wholeness and happiness come with knowing home within us. To feel we are internally anchored in home is what brings the peace, which brings the smile of happiness not only to our face but to our whole body.

Those separated parts that flail around in us and cause us to feel helpless, lost, confused, disconnected and ungrounded are looking to orient to a home base within us. They will run our life until we provide a safe haven of connection for them to return home to. When we establish that space of home base within us so that our separated parts feel secure in moving out of hiding and coming into the light of our life, a home base with connected wholeness inside us is a sacred space of honor and respect for our disconnected parts to return to.

We must first believe that home base exists. Then we can find the space it occupies within us. Most importantly, we must be able to feel trust toward it. At some point, you gave these frightened parts their place of hiding for their protection, to keep them safe and unharmed. At the time you did it, it was the wisest choice you might have known. Often it is an act of youthful innocence, but always the choice results in moving out of connection to the home base within us.

When these parts see that you are in a new relationship with Love and oneness, they will see that they are needed by you for a very different job than protection. In fact, these states of separation want to hold on for dear life to survival mechanisms that are keeping you impotent. Your more expanded sense of self is continually calling these parts back home to your heart and soul's purpose. These parts are being called by your heart and soul through your longing to expand your experience of wholeness and Love. It is your growing strength of connection that calls these parts forth to be seen and healed.

The only way these parts will let go of their old position is to feel they can trust "where" they are going and "who" is responsible for their rearrangement within you, as you. In psychological terms, these separated parts may be seen as the childish parts orienting to the adult self, which is home base. I have found in my many years of spiritual therapy that these childish parts want not just an adult self but a spiritually connected self as their anchor. The only truly secure place for these hungry, "childish" parts is the home base of absolute connection to Spirit found within you. Our connection to Spirit is the true resting place that holds the satisfaction of home base we all long for.

Embodying Home Base

To be in blissful connection to All That Is, feeling the wealth of expanded awareness that is eternal and free, is a fabulous experience. To feel connected to Spirit in its vastness, wholeness and infinite wisdom and Love within our heart and self is our true anchor of home base.

To embody this sense of luscious bliss and have it be available in you're here-and-now life is the key to knowing the abundance we all long for. This is what we hold as the dynamic of home base within. We are designed to embody Spirit and richness in our physical experience. That is our soul purpose and reason for being here.

We embody home base by bringing our experience of connection to Spirit and Love into our heart and cells. We can breathe into our sacred heart whatever symbolizes, or carries, a sense of connection to us, a visual, sensation, feeling, color or sound so that we can establish the look and feel of home base inside that is unique and ever-expanding for us.

As we embody this wealth we open ourselves to living the whole-ness of Love and knowing the assurance of our authentic truth. This is the embodiment of our home base. This is the welcome mat of universal heart we provide for all our lost parts to return to. This soul embodi-ment is necessary to create the place for all the facets of us that have not known the wealth of home to anchor to, integrate with and become the expanded magnet for the wholeness we long to be.

Hope, Trust, Faith, Knowing

To bring our reunion with our soul and its connection to the plen-titude of eternal creative possibilities into our life experience we must have a spiritual sense that this state of abundance is indeed possible. Then we must declare that this state of abundance is truly what we choose to live by.

For many, the experience of connection to the higher dimensions becomes a primary goal to attain. To reach the essence of peace, power, joy and bliss becomes the purpose for meditation, group ritual and worship. To reach sacred heights of touching these qualities of Spirit is a wondrous experience.

I have worked with people for years who have touched these states in deeply memorable ways. They have come to me filled with a sense that the universe is a magical place to behold. They have spoken of reveling in these sensations during moments of stillness, or at the feet of a teacher who has opened that door of divinity while in his or her presence. Many have shared with me their sense of being deeply connected in profound moments in their lives. And still they come to me because they are not satisfied. It is not enough for them to have these heightened sacred moments and then feel they must return to their lives that do not carry this sense of connection. It is my privilege to assist them to go beyond touching the hem of the garment of their divinity to actually embodying the profound nature of creation into their life. They want to *live* from these blissful places in life so the profound and miraculous are daily occurrences. This connection to Spirit is naturally meant to be an ongoing force in their journey, heralding in aliveness, abundance and Love in countless ways.

I salute and celebrate this longing to embody what we touch when we are connected to Spirit's majesty, for this is an essential ingredient to our experience of soul reunion. Our soul is always connected to everything, everywhere.

Our longing to know this connection in our lives is a genuine one. It resides in the blueprint of our DNA and cells. We know we are Spiritual beings having a human experience, but we have not known how to acquire a proficiency in letting our Spirit and form unite in our daily functioning. The ability to have a unified experience in body, mind, heart and soul is the challenge of our times. Having the longing and meeting this challenge in easy, satisfying ways is the purpose of this book.

One important means for bringing Spirit into form is through walking the continuum of hope, faith, trust and knowing as a direct experience of the deepening of Spirit's place in ourselves.

Hope

Hope is the idea, the opening, the light of possibility shining in the darkness. It holds the feeling that there is a better way. When you use the word hope in a sentence you can sense that there is a window or the opening that exists in the realm of possibility, in the field beyond you that you are connected to. The sentence, "I hope to find my lost dog. He ran away yesterday," feels like it hovers in a field that is open and bright, but lacking assurance in its outcome. I liken this to the state of wishing or hoping for peace or oneness. It does indeed hold a ray of sunlight. And it exists in the etheric field beyond one's control. The opening is vital, but it keeps our connection to what we wish to create merely in the arena of possibility.

Trust

Trust is the next rung on the ladder of bringing Spirit into form. Trust holds a beautiful connection to the unseen dimension where all of creation begins. If I have trust I will find my dog I am saying that I believe in a power greater than myself that is involved in creation here and I am unified with it in my mind. When you feel what part of you is engaged when you say, "I trust I will find my dog," you are beholding a union between Spirit and your mind.

Faith

Faith resides primarily in our heart. When I say, "I have faith I will find my dog," I am speaking from a heart that is open to creating from the perspective of Spirit. Through an act of faith we are bringing our connection to Spirit into the realm of possibility and our heart is engaging and participating in any creative outcome. We have a deeper felt sense of union with Spirit's movement through us, as when we declare our faith.

Knowing

Knowing is the place of complete union to Spirit in every cell in us, its grand, expansive nature moving through us. If "I know I will find my dog," every part of me is engaged with Spirit and its creation. This goes beyond possibility, beyond desire, and even beyond holding a special place in the heart for the outcome desired. In knowing there is no separation between Spirit and form, between body and soul, between creator and creation.

When we hold this deep place of knowing, we are free from anything we imagine might keep us from our desired outcome. Intention or hope still carry loopholes of possibility that something might go wrong or leave space for our fears to manifest. Trust still leaves space for uncertainty in our ability to have and hold complete union with peace and Love. Faith keeps our heart sustaining a place for Spirit's bounty, but leaves our conviction in our ability to create from a place of union open for subconscious discussion. True knowing resides deep within our being and cells, guiding our feelings and actions toward a desired outcome.

In knowing, we abide in the sacred space of Spirit's absolute movement in and through us. As we know in every aspect of us an abiding presence of that peace and Love that ignites our lifeblood, we will bring our connection to all the blissful states of Spirit into our daily life. We will hold a knowing conviction to the joy of being alive that is our birthright. We will bring a sense of assurance in ourselves that we can create anything we choose as an extension of our union with the endless qualities of Spirit we are unified with.

Knowing reunion with Spirit is the true power that allows us to know that we are plugged in, tapped in, turned on by all that is sacred and all that is true. There is no room for fear or doubt to find a place in us.

As I speak of the facets of separation within us that keep us being held outside of the grace of infinite Love, remember that to truly know the grace of infinite Love, we must know in our very bone marrow that

Spirit reigns in our heart, our soul and our sense of self. This knowing genuinely establishes the home base that allows all those facets of separation to easily be reunited with the divine presence we long to embody.

The Colors of Separation

The ultimate cause of all maladies, physical, mental or emotional, is the blockage of the flow of Spirit. Maladies are due to the choice to be separated or hold ourselves separate from the all-embracing beloved All That Is.

I am now giving you a feel for how our emotions can truly be seen from the perspective of Spirit. These emotions are simply aspects of ourselves in separation playing out as common patterns we call emotions.

Patterns of Separation

Patterns of separation manifest through our mental and emotional bodies. Bringing these patterns into awareness begins the process of integrating them into our sacred heart and soul. As we walk in the field of separation that we have produced in ourselves, the bottom line for us is the journey out of separation to the home base of connection. Our purpose is to embody All That Is. As we magnify our embodiment of All That Is within us, the facets of separation in us dissolve. As we keep connection to the Divine, that union is expanded in our life experience more than fear and helplessness.

The only way to fully integrate the aspects of us that we have held out from Love is to acknowledge that these emotions hold us hostage to separation and do not allow us to know union and wholeness through the Divine. Then these aspects of us can be freed to be part of the expanded home base needed to explore the abundance of creation we are so eager to explore.

Guilt

There is a built-in alarm system that goes off when we feel guilt. It is meant to be an honest reminder that we are out of integrity with our truth and disconnected from our knowing that being true to our divine self is our only purpose. When we feel guilt it is the signal that we are experiencing our original "sin" of disconnection. The guilt we currently feel stems from the original point of our departure from Spirit, and our rejection of Love when it first happened. At that point we chose to go down the rabbit hole of emotional reactions to our choice for separation versus simply choosing to reclaim our connection. We might have felt guilt about our behavior, and rightly so. If we had recognized the guilt as a signal of separation from our integrity with Spirit we could have simply recognized our misstep in direction and gotten reconnected again. Instead, we let guilt and further judgment and compounded emotions become our God, and direction. All these emotions and stories became our identity, therefore separation became our identity. For most patterns of separation, a habit of trusting the mind begins and we assuage our sense of guilt for having disconnected in the first place. This takes us further from the guidance of heart and soul and away from reconnection. The farther away we get the more guilt we feel for being so far from the home base of union with our spiritual heritage.

Scarcity

The lack of connection to the eternal, limitless resource of Spirit creates the emotional pain of scarcity. Feeling scarcity in relation to any kind of resource, whether it is financial or emotional, is due to cutting off the creative field connected to that resource. For instance, the creative field for money is composed of abundance, success, quality of life and so on. If we are feeling a sense of scarcity in relationship to our ability to generate money in our life, we are cut off from those qualities money represents to us. We do not have receptor sites for those qualities and so we feel scarce in relationship to them. If we are feeling scarce, lack and limitation have been our influences.

Scarcity leads us to believe that merely surviving is enough, that we are lucky just to manage our movement and outcome in life. When we are in the world of scarcity, God is often seen as the one to blame for our rotten state. But how could the one true power place limitations on our ability to create? That is a belief that stems from the space of scarcity.

Depression

Depression is an overload from many aspects of self feeling the burden of separation and not feeling they have the wherewithal to step out of their dilemma. Depression is the result of emotions producing an experience of being held captive within the confines of separation that have taken command of one's life. Depression can feel like a choir of voices crying out in unison. When separation and a consequent lack of life become a common denominator in a number of your facets for expression, you can lose sight of how to reclaim life support for yourself.

Step by step, each aspect must state its need and longing, and bring it into connection with the abundance of Love from the sacred heart. The courage and strength of the connected soul will unravel the burden of these aspects that have been "pressed out of" your expression of life.

Self-Esteem

Lack of self-esteem comes from the shame of knowing we have disconnected from our beloved source. We feel undeserving of Love and support. We may feel unseen or not understood. We don't feel that anyone is watching out for us or even cares. We don't feel worthy of being honored or respected.

We may keep attempting to feel a greater sense of self-esteem by looking for others to make us feel good about ourselves. But no one else can fill the void inside. Asking others to play God to us will never reunite us with our true God within, connected to All That Is.

Low self-esteem reflects the inability to hold infinite Love and creative power within us. It keeps us from drawing on the qualities of Spirit we need each moment to live our life purpose. The solution to low self-esteem is simple. Start to take in those qualities you feel you are lacking by looking in the direction of Spirit for them, rather than from someone or something outside yourself. Your sacred heart and soul are connected to the field of all creation. As you become a living receptor site connected to all creation, you expand into it, carrying the radiant assurance of being a creator of your life and so much more. These qualities are united within you. You are alive with a sense that you are Love connected to all creation.

Shame and Embarrassment

Shame comes in many permutations. There's humiliation, embarrassment, wanting to hide, and wanting to be invisible. Shame can be held so tightly that we even want to be dead rather than see what occurred that we are ashamed of.

Most often it relates to being ashamed of a particular behavior. A feeling of disbelief can accompany shame, which is felt as, "I can't believe I behaved that way." It feels like something very vital and real is being lost. It feels like a large price is going to have to be paid, or a consequence will be put in one's way that is unwelcome.

All this stems from a sense of being ashamed that we were not being true to ourselves, and embarrassed that we did not listen to our inner soul voice. It was available to guide us with assurance but we made a different choice. If you felt the universal support of infinite Love with you, your choice of actions would have been clean and true, with nothing to be ashamed of. So next time a part of you voices its sense of shame for a given act or thought, let it be brought into the light of your connected self, residing in your heart. Feel that place of truth giving voice to what is authentic for you. Simply forgive yourself for not being aligned and let that aspect wanting to hide away in shame return to the light of acceptance and then alignment.

Greed

Greed is the need to acquire based on trying to fill the void created by separation. This greed shows itself not just as a greed for outer acquisitions, but also for love and attention, for instance. It can morph into an obsessive desire for false nourishment of many kinds, all of which are outside of infinite Love.

Hatred

When we become afraid of Love, or power, we might build a wall of hatred toward everything that reminds us that we are separate from divine presence in our experience.

We might hate someone because we choose to guard ourselves against being hurt by them, or we might hate to feel a sense of power from someone or something. That something could be a political party or any system we feel has power in our world. We might hate our body because it reminds us that we have lost command of our life, and we let something other than life force feed or nurture us. Connection to the power of Love melts any hatred.

Security and Insecurity

The nature of willpower, force and grasping to hold onto life, all stem from patterns of insecurity. The need to feel secure in our outer circumstances is indeed a pattern of separation. All these efforts to feel secure result from the sensation that comes from not being connected to the universal pulsation that is filled with all the life resources we could ever imagine.

Joy is the place of true security. Feel joy in your heart and body and notice how secure you feel in knowing that all is abundantly well. You feel wealthy on all levels because you feel one with limitless resources for creation radiating through you. That is true security.

Regret

Simply put, regret comes from the feeling that we missed something, or missed out on some experience. Ultimately, that something that we feel regret about is our experience of missing out on living from the place of connection we know as home. When we feel, for instance, that we regret how we handled a situation or connected with a person, we can know that it is our regret for not holding our absolute connection to the truth of Love in that moment.

Manic States

Manic states are produced when true aliveness is not known. False euphoric states are produced that usually stem from an overriding, over-stimulated, out-of-control fight-or-flight mechanism. Once again, the only remedy for this state of false aliveness is to embody the missing link: authentic aliveness, born from the connection to all life.

Tiredness

An image or sensation that describes the sense of tiredness looks like a blanket that has been placed over several separated aspects. Those aspects are usually proclaiming that they are choosing to hide, not wanting to be seen, heard or engaged. This can relate to not wanting to move forward with greater conviction into a larger world of influence.

To help bring tiredness out of hiding to the height of reconnection and wholeness, bring awareness to what is underlying the feeling of tiredness. Go into the sensation of tiredness and deeply contact those aspects in you that are at a choice point in relationship to expanded, more vibrant life.

Fear

Fear comes from not knowing how to get reconnected to what gives us life. Fear comes when we begin to believe we can't get back home. The basic fear is that we will not be able to return to the home base of spiritual connectedness and feel that presence of Spirit in our heart and in our life.

Fear is the greatest obstacle to accessing your soul's radiance and feeling the sense of home we can know when we reside in our sacred heart. There is no room for Spirit to feed us when we are constricted in fear. Fear may disguise itself as many things, such as concern, control or even measures of safety. But at the core fear is the most insidious inhibitor there is. Fear can leave you completely unglued or paralyzed. It can suck the life out of the bravest of us all.

The key job for fear is to protect us at all costs, or so we believe. To protect us from what? When we are in fear we imagine that we need protection from our perceived dangers. These dangers, interestingly enough, are different for everyone. We buy into them with the idea that the fear will protect us and keep us safe from harm. The fact is that the state of fear in the body and heart is a constriction which shortchanges our ability to receive the absolute knowing that all is well. This knowing only comes from connection to infinite Love—the true power. Fear is the biggest danger, the greatest enemy, because fear's job is to keep us from life and freedom. It keeps us from being in command of our life. It is the greatest weapon of mass destruction, for it has created all war and furthered the dimension of separation on this planet in countless ways.

We live out of fear if we imagine that we are limited in some way. We are afraid we aren't in command of our life. We fear that we won't be allowed to create what we want in relationship to our immediate needs or in relationship to the outcome of our life, in the short term and long term. It's true, when we step into fear we have made a virtual lockdown on free choice. When we feel we have no choice we resort to control. We only feel the need to control when our connection to Love is not present.

In short, when fear is present, it is simply the manifestation of some facet in us not knowing its way home, unsure of its anchor. This facet is afraid that we will not help it return home. Our job is to give it Love, direction and support to find its way home so it may return to be part of Love and wholeness. It is vital to remind that aspect that fear itself is what keeps it in separation, holding a sense of being incapable of spiritual reunion.

What makes the ride on the amusement park of life so terrifying is our state of separation. Being outside of connection to our true nature, which is connected to all of creation, is a scary ride indeed. When we feel fear in our life, what we are saying in essence is that without connection we don't know how to handle life.

Fear of Coming Into Life

One particular root of fear that has soul-level origins is the fear of coming into life. It is not that we are afraid to come into life itself. We are afraid of coming into life without the resources of Spirit we need.

We translate the fear of coming into an incarnation into a fear of stepping into our immediate personal life. We are afraid to experience the sensation of life. Our fear of engagement produces a sense of being withdrawn, pulled back or depressed. Our main focus may be on managing our survival. This powerless state is often coupled with a fight-or-flight, hypervigilant mechanism established to defend against perceived dangers. Our state of fight or flight births a sense of false aliveness. Underneath is a growing separation from Spirit that makes us feel increasingly fearful of existing. This experience of separation can even leave us with the feeling that life and Spirit have abandoned us.

It is not life you are afraid of, but being separate from life that makes you afraid.

It is freeing to reconnect those fearful parts of ourselves to the field of creation. When our fear is reunited to the power of Love it is transformed to the sense of magic that all things are possible. We are free to engage the way we wish, for we, not our fear, are once again in command.

Fear Giving Way to Freedom

Often a man who is feeling stressed from work is feeling that he is not being given the chance to feel the sense of freedom he craves within the constraints of his work situation. Freedom, as a quality of Spirit, is very important to the forward movement of masculine energy. Freedom to vision, dream, expand, see new possibilities and to be in command of life is what masculine energy thrives on. Women hold a masculine energy as well. We all have the longing to live with the freedom of Spirit. For the following, I am using a scenario that is common in men.

A man who feels constricted deep in his soul often does not feel free in his life, whether in a work situation or in the context of his home life. He might feel compelled to get away from it all to cultivate his need for freedom. There is nothing wrong with that urge. It is quite natural to want to leave our current outer rhythm to breathe fresh air, for space and deepening connection, or simply for joy and fun. He is listening to the longing of his heart to expand his experience of life.

On the other hand, if we don't feel free in a situation because we feel fearful or powerless, leaving the situation might be avoiding our fear and powerlessness. This way of gaining freedom becomes a Band-Aid for a wound that will never go away.

The only true way to experience freedom is to feel free in ourselves within any or all situations we are in. The only way to feel this is to tap into the expanse of universal freedom. Then we don't have anything to be free from. We are free to create in accordance with the universal prin-

ciples of truth and integrity that coexist with universal freedom. They
are not separate, in fact. We find we are not bound by circumstances
because we are not afraid of them, nor do we feel powerless in them.

Limitation Birthing Freedom

Christopher Reeve provided us with a vivid example of a man
with extreme outer limitations who was charged with a ferocity to live.
This ferocity to live birthed a freedom to create what he was passionate
about. He is an example of spiritual connection forging true freedom.
Nelson Mandela is certainly another example. He lived in solitary con-
finement, the most locked-down outer situation one could imagine. His
Spirit soared and he emerged a truly free man from the inside out, to
contribute the power of authentic freedom to transform this world in
countless ways. There are endless examples.

When you live in the magic of creation, you touch the realm of limitless possibilities for answers, solutions and creative genius. This activates
a force field for vital, vibrant, potent and adventurous movement that is
self-initiated in even the most dire situations. No matter how bleak the
situation might appear, staying open in heart, soul and body to Love and
the sacred heart makes even the unimaginable possible.

A beacon of light in the recent Haitian earthquake of 2010 was
the ceaseless singing in prayer by those who lived through it. This
singing was in high contrast to the fear we might have imagined the
victims of the earthquake had every right to express. Fear and victimhood do not answer prayers, only our openhearted, knowing
connection to Spirit opens the heavens for divine participation. There
is no state of bondage in us that Spirit cannot masterfully unlock and
release when we are open to its penetration. A beautiful example of
this was shown on national news. A woman who was buried under
rubble for six days said, when she was pulled out, that she just kept
singing. She knew she wasn't going to die. She was singing even
when she was rescued and pulled out of what could have been her
burial place.

Fear of the Unknown

How does the fear of the unknown that moves through our subconscious like a snake, this fear that seems to run us in so many unseen and unknown ways, relate to our separation from Spirit?

Fear of the unknown directly relates to the sensation of not having Spirit within us as our guiding light. It is the fear we knew when we originally separated from Source and hurled ourselves into the space that separation generates. It was completely unknown and unfamiliar. Many of us felt a sense of devastation and "lostness," as though we had just experienced an earthquake or tornado and lost everything. We felt we had absolutely nothing to hold on to. All of us have experienced this fear because we have all experienced separation to varying degrees.

So no wonder the fear of the unknown has such an instant sense of trauma in our cellular, even soul, memory banks. It links us to that initial experience of separation, wherever that was, however that looked for each of us.

We are deeply afraid of the unknown because the thought of increasing that sensation of separation in us is horrific at some unseen level. It is coupled with the fear of being out of control, which being separate also produces. In the state of separation our home is nowhere to be found. We are not in command of ourselves because we have allowed something beyond ourselves to be in charge.

We don't trust ourselves to freely move, fueled by Spirit, because we don't trust our ability to make clear choices and decisions. All it takes is one step out of alignment into separation, to begin to distrust ourselves.

If we are disconnected, we have every reason to feel unsure about our future, whether that pertains to the next five minutes or the next ten years. Everything feels unknown, for light is not shining on our movement. It's hard to trust the lack of light, which fear of the unknown inherently carries. When disconnected, we are separate from the power, support, magic and vibrancy we need for creating the next moment. We are left with the grip of having to survive. Our resources are limited to willpower and fight-or-flight techniques to manage our life.

I liken our fear of the unknown, and our subsequent mistrust of ourselves, to hanging on to the side of the pool when we first learn to swim. We are hanging on for dear life while wondering why our life is not opening in the ways we want it to. Hanging on is a fear mechanism that is meant to provide safety. Only by letting go of the side of the pool and swimming into the waters of life will we have the abundant resources of the field of all creation.

Our hesitation about moving into a realm we call "the unknown" also stems from our belief that we don't trust that abundant life is always ready to welcome us with open arms. If we are disconnected, we imagine the space we are moving into will continue to be disconnected. Only when we are aligned with infinite Love can we feel and trust that our life will be held by infinite Love in each moment.

Invulnerability

When we are feeling a fear of the unknown we may feel vulnerable to factors in our environment and feel out of control in relation to our surroundings and the people in it. I often have people say to me that they are afraid to be vulnerable. They are afraid of being exposed or open to others and the world around them. It is not wise to blindly expose ourselves to those around us if we are not first connected to Love and our own inner sense of home base. When we feel that others are responsible for our well-being we will unnaturally expose ourselves to them and then regret that we feel vulnerable to our outside world. When we are expecting that the world will take care of us we set ourselves up to believe that we must be vulnerable to others in order to be taken care of. Then, when we feel we won't be taken care of, or have been abandoned, we regret feeling vulnerable, or exposed, and pull in with fear of bringing our self and our gifts to others and into the world. That is a highly probable consequence in the space disconnected from infinite Love. We have abandoned our true place of connectedness. It follows that we avoid being vulnerable to people and situations for a reason. We are not meant to be vulnerable to the world.

> **Vulnerability is a means of staying open to the embrace of infinite Love.**

If you are afraid of being vulnerable, you become invulnerable. Avoiding being vulnerable is embracing being invulnerable, in fact. Availing yourself to the true sense of vulnerability is vulnerability to Spirit's pulsation and its embodiment within you. Invulnerability, or the inability to be penetrated, keeps you in the state of being cut off and you don't feel supported and a part of the world. You become out of touch and more afraid to engage because you aren't open to connect.

If we are afraid of being vulnerable in relationship to others, we will protect ourselves, thinking this will keep us from getting hurt. Our protection mechanisms cut off our vulnerability. It may appear to our mind that not to be vulnerable is a good thing. Our internal space of vulnerability is an essential space for us to hold sacred, so that we are always open to Spirit and have receptor sites within our heart for it. If we protect ourselves, even from the idea of being hurt, we are constricting our sacred receptor space for Spirit. No wonder we feel we could be in danger.

> **When a wall of protection is in place, we are constricting our entrance, not just to danger, but to everything. This includes Love, and all qualities of Spirit we wish to receive.**

When we are open to be supported and held sacred by Spirit, we are vulnerable to our union with the beloved All That Is. Only when we allow Spirit to penetrate our existence can we know our absolute anchor in universal power. Vulnerability to that is easy. This vulnerability is rich and holds many rewards. Vulnerability creates a space for the larger capacity of Spirit to embrace us. It allows us to explore the abundant treasures in the infinite field of creation. We dwell in the space that knows God is in Love with the essence of who we are. True vulnerability leaves no room for fear or powerlessness, for in that open and anchored place we are in full contact with what guides and ignites our being.

Feeling Alone, Fear of Being Alone

Melissa was having difficulty with her partner and wanted a soul perspective around their relationship and if they should stay together. She really wanted to truly know within herself what was real and true for her in this matter. She shared with me that her heart hurt every time she thought of not being with Jim. This really confused her sense of clarity around knowing which direction the relationship should take.

I had her go deeply into this pain in her heart for a moment so she could allow herself to fully feel the nature of the density, the texture, the breadth of the pain. I reminded her that the pain was living in her physical heart not her sacred heart. We spoke about the fact that she had created this pain. She had created it as a warning within herself when someone's outer behavior would trigger her to remind her not to open her heart any further. It was a warning of danger and told her to back off.

As she realized this she felt safe to go into this pain in her heart, sensing it as being more her own creation than a devastating pattern too scary to go into. Then she felt a deep fear of being alone that she was terrified to even go near.

We surrounded that precious scared part with light, scooped it up into her loving hands, and brought it into her sacred heart. It had every right to be holding a deep sense of feeling alone. It had been held out in separation from Love for a long time. Its job had been to sense a potential danger. It had no way of being part of her sacred heart's connection to oneness and infinite Love.

Together we sensed a collective presence beginning to exude from her sacred heart and then it surrounded her. The feeling of eternal,

unconditional Love and support was palpable. She was smiling and crying tears of relief, release and joy. She laughed as she told me she heard
a few phrases from a Michael Jackson song: "You are not alone. I am at
your side." She said that she truly felt this abiding presence as a precious
gift to this part that felt so desperately alone and so afraid of being alone.
Her physical heart melted into union with her sacred heart and she felt
a huge sense of coming home.

As she held this place of connection to the infinite Love in her heart
and this collective presence of Love all around her, she knew that it was
okay for her to let go of this relationship that was not feeding her. Her
fear of being alone did not have to keep her in an unhealthy relationship
with Jim. She felt a calm assurance in herself that Love was present and
would assist her to sort out the details of this life transition. I reminded
her that her "success" in this transition was directly related to her conviction to hold this infinite Love in her heart throughout her day. Then
she would be in cocreation with Love as she walked this path that was
hers to walk. She could now do it free of her fear of being alone at the
helm. Now that she had infinite Love solidly within her, she could trust
that she would create outer partnerships in her life born of the sacred
space of Love she held above all else.

The Creative Void

When we are afraid of the unknown, we are afraid of stepping into
the natural creative void that continually exists. The creative void is
a necessary step in the creative process. It holds the dynamic of free
choice. In each moment we are declaring and radiating light, or we are
choosing to declare our support to the lack of light. The creative void
is necessary for the individuated manifestation of creation through us.
Connecting to this void allows us to be in command of how we will let
light create through us.

If you feel fear of the unknown, you can change your perspective.
Visualize yourself moving into a creative void. Because you are in com-

mand of life for yourself in every moment declare, "Let there be light now." You have just transformed your fear of the unknown to a state of being in the known with readiness to cocreate with light.

You can begin to relax, trust and have a deep sense of knowing that the space that seems unknown is filled with Spirit, Love and unity. You value this space of union with Spirit to such a degree that the fear of the so-called unknown dissolves. You awaken to the knowledge that you live in the world of Spirit—by choice.

Helplessness

The feeling of helplessness is prolific in the state of separation. We feel helpless anytime we feel our heart and soul are not there to guide us. We feel helpless when we don't know how to return to our inner sense of home.

> **We feel helpless when we are seeking outside ourselves for Love and power because nothing outside ourselves can ever fulfill our need for connection.**

Our only true need or longing is for connection to Spirit that gives us the resources we need to fuel our life. When we are immersed in a sense of being paralyzed with fear, out of control or not in command, feelings of helplessness find an easy resting place in us. And we begin to feel justified in our right to play victim.

If we are disconnected and trying to survive by our little will, or fight or flight, we will feel ineffectual and helpless to make the changes we want. A feeling of overwhelm precedes helplessness or comes quickly on its heels. Separation causes helplessness; there is no place to turn for real help when we are disconnected from genuine support and assistance.

Helplessness is feeling we have to fight for our life when we are in a frame of mind that says we have no support, Love, guidance, direction or strength. For instance, if we are using our personal will to find a new job and saying, "I *will* find a job," hiding behind that push is an aspect that feels helpless to create what it truly longs for. So force of will tries to override this sense of helplessness. From this stance, the universe is not being given a space to cocreate a great job with you.

To turn around the state of helplessness you must ask for help. You are feeling helpless—lacking help. When we ask for assistance from Spirit we are asking to move out of "poor little helpless me" into being creator of our world, unified with the field of all creation.

Helen had an ovarian cyst that appeared very quickly. She'd already had one cyst removed and the subsequent scan initially showed no more cysts forming. Then a week later, there was a new one. In our session together, Helen let herself go into this area of her body with the new cyst, knowing that with my assistance she was ready to release this pattern of separation her body was holding in the cyst. It was obviously screaming to get her attention.

As Helen put her attention on the area where she could feel the cyst, she heard it crying out to her helplessly, "Help me out." Then it said it was feeling attacked and helpless.

"Who or what wants to help this part?" I asked.

"Love from my heart and my husband's strength and protection," she said. Then she felt those qualities of Spirit pour into the area of the cyst. She let that aspect that was calling for help, that felt it was being held hostage in the cyst, open and receive the Love and strength at its own pace, until they were united. That aspect stopped crying out. It felt a rush of loving assistance and support, warmth and relaxation.

A week later she learned at a doctor's appointment the cyst had disappeared. The aspect of Helen that was creating a cyst filled with the helplessness of feeling attacked dissolved during its union with Love and strength of connection. As the pattern of feeling attacked and helpless got the Love and support it needed it could release its grip of fear and helplessness and be reunited with its part in creating, not protecting. There was no need to hold the pattern to bring this aspect of separation to her attention. It was reunited with Spirit. The cyst dissolved and the feeling of Love and strength expanded in this powerful place of creation held in her uterus.

A key in the cyst disappearing was that Helen was not involved in undoing the block but in resourcing what she needed to answer the cry for connection to the qualities of Spirit. The cyst dissolved when Spirit, as life force holding Love and strength, was reclaimed. When Spirit's strength was reclaimed the cyst dissolved. This strength was never absent, it was just let go of at some point and replaced with a feeling of being victim to a perceived attack.

Powerlessness

Anger is an emotional reaction to the sensation of feeling powerless. It is also a way to try to feel more alive, when we aren't feeling alive. It is an emotion of false aliveness. Feeling powerless is the by-product of separation. We experience powerlessness when we are acting from a personal will that is not connected to the will of the sacred heart and soul. Personal will creates destruction and disruption and it produces power struggles. All power struggles are born from a place of powerlessness.

When we feel powerlessness it's easy to move into helplessness and hopelessness. The heart constricts and our spiritual resources become cut off. We are not creating a space for help or support. We feel powerless to change the situation.

To come out of powerlessness or helplessness and begin to take charge of our life, we may use anger to help push ourselves out of a rut. This is a misuse of power, but it is often a step out of the powerlessness from separation to the true power of presence we carry when we are embodying our spiritual strength. Power that is a false high is impotent. Also, power that is not aligned with creation is destructive. When you find yourself dealing with anger, remember that below its surface is the feeling of powerlessness and helplessness. Both stem from separation. True power is the power of Love, the power of peace and the power of courage. All of these facets of true power must be born of Spirit and brought forth in our physical dimension. As we see our anger for what it is, we are allowing our angry parts to be seen, reunited and reclaimed within the field of true power. Then our Spirit feels meaning and purpose and a passion and fuel for creation. Our primary responsibility is to ensure creation's participation through us. That is the true power of enacting our soul purpose.

Mental Confusion

When we say, "I don't know," or "I don't know how," or "I don't see a clear path or have direction or purpose," we can be sure our mind is in separation from our heart and our soul. For example, you don't know how to go about finding a new job. You are confused about whether your girlfriend is right for you. You can't resolve an issue with your child or your computer. You simply feel confused, unclear or lost in your mind. These are patterns of separation.

You can't resolve these patterns at the level where they are hung up, which is in the mind.

Reconnection to the true source for any direction or purpose, any clarity of movement is always the key. Here's a simple, elegant reframe for doubts in our minds. Without connection to Spirit, I don't know how to do it. Without a connection to Spirit, I don't see a clear path, direction or purpose. Clarity is clearly stating the truth of your mental confusion.

I Can't Do This

So often we feel a cry inside that says, "I can't do this." This can relate to enduring physical pain, emotional pain, feeling incapable, overwhelmed or paralyzed in fear. That is a true cry from an aspect of us that genuinely feels clueless, helpless and hopeless. It might feel like a *very* large part of us.

It is crying out from the pain of separation saying, "I can't do 'this' without Spirit. I can't do this without Love. I can't live this way anymore without the help of connection to the divine guidance I have cut myself off from."

In these situations you want your mantra to be: "I can't do this (whatever it is) without reuniting with Spirit to find the way through, to find the light at the end of the tunnel, to know that Love does exist. I can't do this without my heart and soul connection to Spirit moving in me now, in the midst of the challenging situation I am in."

With this reframe you are declaring that you, as reconnected you, are in cocreative command. You are available to bring reunion to those aspects of your experience that have become mired in separation and are crying to live from the power of creation again. Spirit connects us to the realm of infinite possibilities and the strength to know how to create from those abundant resources anytime.

Living Beyond Our Means

As I am writing this book, the United States and the rest of the world are in a challenging time that is being named a recession. This recession stems largely from our uncontrolled habit, individually and collectively, to live beyond our means. Everyone can see ways that he or she has lived beyond their means. Financially it is obvious in dollars and cents. If the means for generating financial abundance is not coming from a connection to universal abundance, then we are living beyond our means. At the level of the physical body, health problems stem from living beyond our means. We are attempting to use our body without being connected with life force. We do not have the fuel to generate what we are asking our bodies to do for us.

Relationship issues often point to the tendency to live beyond our means in regards to our hearts and our capacity to hold Love. When we try to relate to another and our tank is empty, and we ask another to fill us in various ways, we are living beyond our means. If your heart and sense of self is filled with infinite Love, you have the means to cocreate with others. That is living within your means.

Living beyond our means magnifies the state of separation we live in. It reveals when we are attempting to live without Spirit at the helm of our life.

How do we solve our individual problems, our country's mess and our world's lack of unity with connection to Love and creation? It starts with each one of us reuniting with Spirit in the places we have lived without it.

Sadness, Grief, Loss

Sadness and grief, which are triggered by an event involving loss, appear to be connected to a deep well of never-ending pain. This bottomless pit we tap in to seems to carry a sadness that is entirely disproportionate to the situation. Fear of hitting this bottomless pit keeps us frozen. We avoid what we believe will make us fall into it and forever lose something we value.

Our deep grief that springs from events of loss becomes part of our cellular and DNA memory. But there is also a part of grief which belongs to a soul-level feeling of loss of connection to infinite Love. The heartache each of us has brought from that loss of connection is a devastating state to delve into. It often comes with a deep sense of helplessness in overcoming the loss of connection to all that matters in our core and sacred heart.

Allison spoke with me just after she had tapped into a heart-wrenching sense of loss around Easter. She was feeling her inability to love and be loved. She realized that it was the sense of loss of "Christ Love," as she described it, that had an undeniably stable and powerful presence for her. Her sense of grief for the loss of that Love was almost too much for her to bear. We discovered during past lives and times as a soul that she was in a situation that prevented her from being able to experience the divine nature of Christ Love. In those times, if she had spoken of her devotion or even carried that Love in her heart, she was condemned for it. I helped her unravel her pattern of separation from Love and the grief she held. She drank in her reunion with divine Christ Love. As we were in this process we brought to light the fact that each time she participated in being prevented from knowing Christ Love she had shut her heart a little more. She thought this was the prudent move in the face of these perpetrators. Her heart suffered the most and her soul and DNA carried this pattern of protective closure with her. Each time she felt the potential that she might be hurt or lose her ability to know Love, she would, in prevention, close her heart. So her heart's capacity to be a receptor site for Love became smaller and smaller. She was the one responsible for closing off Love, not the perpetrators. So the grief for the loss of connection became bigger and deeper.

The truth is that grief and sadness are the body's mechanisms to keep the heart supple and open, to be available to Love. In a time of tears or sadness, your heart may actually hurt. It is the heart's way of saying, "I'm cracking open. I want to be open and available again to Love. I want to reunite with my true nourishment. Through me, let Love come into my soul and body. Let me be alive and welcome Love again."

Whenever we feel a sense of sadness and grief, loss or emptiness, it is the heart longing and aching for reunion with its Beloved: infinite Love. All Allison had to do was apologize to her heart and soul and every aspect of herself that she had withheld from Love. She forgave herself for having separated from Love in the first place. Then her heart could expand, and weep as it released the bondage it had held, and could now cry in joy for its reunion with Love. She then proclaimed absolute loyalty to and oneness with the Christ presence that freely and joyfully pulsed through her heart and whole being. She was back on track with her original soul purpose: to bring Christ Love into the world because *she* held it sacred. Now others could know Love existed because she held its sacred presence radiating naturally from her.

A Heart Held Open to Love

When the human heart cries out, no matter what it feels it is lacking, it is always calling out to be reunited with Love. Keeping the sacred heart open to Love is essential and always possible, regardless how painful the circumstance is. When the sacred heart stays connected and full, there is no loss or grief to experience.

It's common to think that in the face of a potential attack it is expected, even required, for the heart to protect, armor or close. Often when we are feeling deep grief or loss we think we are being "attacked" by a sense of overwhelm and helplessness combined with an inability to get reconnected to stability within ourselves.

If you saw and loved the symbolism in the movie *Braveheart* as much as I did, you probably see that we always have a choice in our heart of how we operate. We can always keep our heart connected to its lifeline of Love no matter what. Know that this act of staying available to Love is the only true choice. At the end of the movie, while William Wallace was drawn and quartered, just before he went unconscious, he yelled, "Freedom!!" Regardless of what was done to his body his Spirit remained free and alive, and his sacred heart and soul were untouched. He showed that it was possible to stay connected to Spirit and he did not have to take any pattern of separation with him, at a heart and soul level, into his next incarnation. Love continued to fuel his soul's existence and therefore his ability to embody it. It is better to let go of your body and maintain divine connection than to hold an empty, abandoned place that feels like it needs to be protected while merely surviving, without infinite Love coursing through your veins.

Fear of Not Being Taken Care of

In our world at the present time, the sense of separation is a large source of pain for many people. Security measures everywhere have elevated in response to a perpetual undercurrent of panic held by the majority of our population since 9/11. A substantial part of this panic stems from the fear that we won't be taken care of. As I mentioned more extensively in the section on "The Invisible Enemy," there is a deep conviction that there is something out there that could take our life in an instant and it's called "the terrorist threat." Never mind that natural disasters and our own poor choices create far more deaths than terrorists. It is our fear that we won't be taken care of that is at the root of these future-oriented fears around potential terrorist attacks, nuclear explosions and any other power we imagine is outside of our control.

Another way our fear of not being taken of shows itself collectively is through the complexity and muckiness of the process of Health Care reform. While ironing out national health care is a gigantic project, at the root of the inability for this vital arena to be given a healthy new beginning or approach, or for health care to even move forward out of its unhealthy state, is this fear that resides in most: "Will I be taken care of? I'm afraid to make or support any changes in health care for fear that it will mean I won't be taken care of." The best way for us to create any system that works is for many of us to reunite with the knowing that we are taken care of by the benevolent, ever-present universal Spirit. Then we must embody that knowing that we are taken care of. As this occurs, we will see reflected in our outer world a beautiful, resourceful system emerging that takes into account the individual and collective right to health and well-being. Complaining about the political process doesn't serve anyone. Once again, union with Spirit is the answer.

Through this pattern of separation we express that we do not trust that there is an all-knowing and all-seeing, eternal presence that holds all of us in the sacred embrace of benevolent life. We don't trust this omnipotent presence of light because we separated from it, and let go of our healthy, knowing relationship with it. So we don't believe we will be taken care of. That is valid, because in separation from the omnipotent presence of light, we are not connected to the source field that will naturally take care of us.

How to cure the fear of not being taken care of? Give to that part of you that is in mistrust the one thing that is utterly trustworthy: Spirit's embrace. As you create within you what you deem trustworthy in the realm of Spirit, it naturally embraces you. Then we know that all is well. And it is.

The law of attraction shows that what we hold inside us manifests. If we hold a mistrust that we won't be taken care of, we won't be taken care of. If we hold and embody a knowing that all is well in the universe we create and inhabit, then all will be well in the universe we inhabit.

To feel taken care of we must know this to be true in our heart and body. The parts that do not feel taken care of must be given the opportunity to be held by Spirit and feel honored, Loved, respected and cherished. When we know we are being taken care of by infinite Love, our world feels held by that level of Love.

Caretaking as a Pattern of Separation

Many women I speak with have completed the stage of caretaking that feels burdensome, obligatory and gives back nothing in return. This kind of caretaking is more than parenting. These women created a sense of martyrdom. Coupled with this is a sense that they give and give, with nothing coming back in return. This is what happens when we take the idea of selfless Love too far.

Often caretaking love is chosen because we have disconnected from infinite Love and want desperately to participate in the realm of Love in one way or another. When we have this kind of motivating personal agenda disguised as giving Love, it sours. When these women are asked if this way of experiencing Love was working, they answer "no." It was not working for them to love others to get love in return in hopes that others would fill their empty hearts.

These same women have had enough of caretaking everyone and everything, but they are afraid of letting go of this way of functioning because they fear they will not have any means for knowing Love.

When we are ready to move out of the fear that we won't be taken care of if we stop caretaking others, we can ask ourselves, "What nature of Love truly fills my heart and soul?" Forgive yourself for settling for caretaking Love and ask for reunion with infinite Love. It exists everywhere universally except in the place in you where you separated from it. It takes true courage to let go of caretaking love and reunite with infinite Love, discovering that it was always there for you.

All of creation awaits our call and welcomes us with open arms.

What About Me?

At some level we are all attention grabbers. What about me? Who is going to take care of me? Who will witness my life and acknowledge my existence? Who will make my life work, while loving me unconditionally? These questions stem from the parts of us that feel disconnected and therefore feel invisible to Spirit. These parts also feel outside of, isolated from, alienated from, life. These patterns of isolation readily turn to blaming those closest to us. When we are in the aspect of ourselves that cries out, "What about me?" we blame someone else for not filling all our needs.

But we are the ones who neglected Spirit. We abused it, misused the power of Love, denied it and disbelieved in it. We let go of and forgot about Spirit. It never forgot about us.

When a part is crying out, "What about me?" it is most often asking in relationship to someone else's failure to see or acknowledge that part.

For example, Elena said to me, "He is so mean. He doesn't care enough about me to see I'm hurting." Elena is actually pushing him away, creating more separation between them. She is pushing him out of her heart and closing the door on it. When she closes the door to her heart, there is no room for him to come in and even attempt to offer his care, Love and support to her. So whose fault is it that she is not being cared for or seen? With a heart closed to Love, she becomes invisible and unavailable.

What if that aspect of Elena that feels unnoticed by someone close to her asks Spirit within her for the connecting link needed to fill her with the qualities of Spirit she is crying out for? Bringing in those qualities of being seen to the place of her heartache will fill her heart with the trust that she can get her needs met. Those around her will feel her open heart, filled with the assurance that she deeply matters. They will magically see her for who she is. As she lets Spirit see and acknowledge her, her fullness of being seen will radiate and be a welcome place for many to cocreate with.

Lack of Intimacy

Lack of intimacy in our relationships comes from our lack of intimacy known in our heart to Spirit and Love. First, we must develop an open, honest, vulnerable, deep and treasured connection with the beloved Spirit from which we were birthed. Then we will easily be able to breathe that intimacy into our relationships with those we choose to share our intimacy of connection to the Beloved.

> **Every breath is an intimate romance with all that is beloved.**

Betrayal

Each of us can identify with the piercing sensation of feeling betrayed. It can feel like a deep blow to our stomach, or a sense of utter shock and collapse. With it comes a devastating sense of loss of self and all we thought we could trust. The feeling sensation is real and intimate.

The only way through this wasp's nest of emotions is to recognize that the pattern of betrayal originated in our betrayal of trust in connection to Spirit. When we separate from Spirit's generosity, wisdom and clarity of guidance, we have betrayed our true compass and true sense of our universal nature. We set up the pattern of weakness as clear as a sign on our chest that says, "I have betrayed my God. I looked outside myself and my union with God to let someone, or something outside myself, play God." We have moved outside ourselves. As soon as we place our trust in a false source of power and guidance, it will surely betray us. It must, so we can remember that the only true allegiance is to our divine nature moving through our heart and soul.

Forgiveness, reunion, reclaiming our true universal nature, is the path home. When we know home, we know it will never forsake us; it will never betray us. We then learn to trust our connection and thus our inner voice that gives expression to that connection. When we declare that we will never betray that, we will never have to experience betrayal again.

Abandonment

Counter to what many say, abandonment issues can go away. Once we take responsibility for our original separation, which was our abandonment of Spirit, we are ninety percent free and clear of the issue.

As we practice living from the wholeness of the embodiment of our soul self, soul gifts and our sacred union with the Beloved, we are filled with the majestic sense of knowing Love and home in ourselves that is never going away. We value it so deeply that we would never imagine abandoning this precious jewel in our crown. We honor and hold sacred that connection, like a prayerful vow.

In the Hawaiian language there is an exquisite word for this feeling of union with this prayerful vow. *Ohana. Ohana* means family and family means no one is left behind or forgotten. Abandonment does not exist when *Ohana*, the Spirit of family within infinite Love, is held.

**Your divine self is always present to bathe you
in the radiance of its connection to magnificent
Love.**

Rejection

If the barnacle on our soul or the pain you are feeling currently, is the sensation of rejection, you can know that it was created by an innocent or deliberate choice to open to something other than absolute connection to infinite Love. In essence, we rejected infinite Love or the universal power of Spirit in that moment. We created the pattern of separation we have subsequently felt as rejection in relationship to Love or true power. When the feeling of rejection arises in an aspect of us, it is longing for reunion. It is crying out to be received into Spirit. It is critical not to reject the feeling of rejection, for this compounds it. As all of our separated parts are received and accepted by us, we experience wholeness. Any time our wound of separation arises as the feeling of rejection, we can know that back of it is our pattern of rejection of Spirit in that facet of our expression. Our beloved universe is always present for us and will never turn its back on us. That is an absolute, or we would not exist.

The question we must ask ourselves, in an ongoing fashion: "Am I available to Love and the power of Spirit's presence, or am I rejecting it right now?"

I Don't Belong Here

Many have a sense that, "This world is not my world. This is not where I belong. I am an alien and I don't feel seen or understood here."

If we, in any aspect of ourselves, have not allowed Spirit to freely inhabit our body, mind and heart, we will feel like we don't belong here. What we are saying in truth is that we don't feel natural in our world if there is any degree of separation. It is not meant to be that way. Without Spirit's influence we have no desire to be here. A soul coming here with all its brilliance and buoyancy could easily feel as though there is no place for it in this dense world filled with a mixture of light and separation from light. The heart cries out, "Is this really what I signed up for?"

In fact, you signed up to bring the light of infinite possibilities available from the field of creation. Certainly, this world, upon first viewing it, or even viewing it from a place of separation today, does not appear to be interested in participating in any plan based on creation. It all appears to most humans to operate out of a survival-based menu of fear, greed, power struggle and victimization. Why would you, as a soul filled with joy and gratitude, choose to participate in all of this? Better to hide or hold back your gifts and take the stance of an alien or a spiritual victim, which proclaims that there is no place for your soul's purposes.

To shed a little more light on the topic, remember that if you chose to hold the stance that you don't belong here, or you feel misunderstood and definitely do not feel received, you are only cutting yourself off from the wealth of universal resources that you are a part of, that you magically fit with. When you feel alienated or misunderstood you have a tendency to withdraw or pull back. You often pull back from everything, and that includes all your life-given resources for thriving and knowing wholeness here.

This whole universe wants you and holds a treasured place for you. It is only a thin layer of human consciousness, separated from Source, that you don't feel a part of. So why throw abundance away because you feel different than the few lost souls here?

It is up to you to create your world. The world you inhabit is indeed a reflection of you. How about bringing in and living from Spirit's magnificence and live from that world, regardless of what others living in separation are experiencing. Are you afraid that you will feel alone and isolated if you live by Spirit's magnificence while the majority here are not? You can see your whole relationship to this world in a completely different light. You can feel alien to the craziness of the pattern of separation that you feel running rampant in the world. You can awaken to belong to the universal oneness that exists everywhere. That is the world, the energy field, the reality you truly belong to and desire to belong to. It is your soul purpose to bring it here. You can then bring this sense of universal belonging to the world because you embody it in yourself, as your world, regardless of what others chose to experience.

It is your job to make a place for "you" here. You get to choose the depth and breadth of that "you" and the expansiveness of your connection to the Divine. Then you discover that this expanded space of connection is truly the real world. Divinity is reality. This is the world you chose to inhabit by deliberately choosing to embody that divinity. Your body is the first point of entrance for your divine self. If it is in you, it is in the world, your world. "Coming back" here to this world, disconnected from oneness, is not coming back to reality, it is coming to the lack of reality.

What you hold to be true in yourself, and especially in your heart, radiates to the whole world.

Simply, elegantly and generously hold your embodiment of Spirit uppermost and ecstasy will arrive at your door. It can't help but do so.

Feeling Limited

When we feel limited we are really saying that we do not feel free. Freedom is an inner state of being. It is much easier and freer to reclaim our aspects that do not feel free than to continually avoid uncomfortable situations to be free from something so we can imagine we're free. Avoiding situations is a powerless and helpless way to be. The only way to truly know freedom is to be connected to the field of limitless possibilities. This is the field that taps us into the support system of all of creation. This field, when we bring it into the creative power center of our abdomen, is essential to let us feel the anchor of universal freedom and absolute connection moving in union within us.

We are then ready to freely create in any moment, when our physical body is filled with the eternal gift of Spirit's wealth.

Go deep beyond even the freedom to make choices, the freedom to speak your truth and the freedom to move in Spirit on this Earth. The deepest freedom we can give ourselves is being one with the field of all creation, one with infinite Love.

> *"Stone walls do not a prison make,*
> *Nor iron bars a cage;*
> *… If I have freedom in my Love*
> *And in my soul, I am free,*
> *Angels alone, that soar above, enjoy such liberty."*
>
> Richard Lovelace: "To Althea, From Prison"

Sexuality

Sexuality often seems to be a cauldron for the wounds of separation to appear. We would be wise to notice that our issues around sexuality relate to parts of ourselves that are not free to fully embody the Divine. Our wounds of separation in relationship to male and female representation of Spirit manifest in sexuality. This is the arena for Spirit and infinite Love to be commanded into physical existence. When we confine Spirit to the invisible world, the physical experience is diminished. When we are not free to embody infinite Love and know that spirituality and sexuality are one, there are aspects of us held out in separation from their divine birthright of knowing sexuality as a physical embodiment of Spirit's wealth. The creation of physicality was designed to celebrate the glory of life.

Sexual experience is the dimension where the greatest ecstasy of Spiritual union through the six senses can be known. This union brings forward the embodiment of all qualities of Spirit we are open to. Our union with our Beloved, as it shows up for each of us, is the most profound experience to be known, rich with the experience of feeling fully alive and even ecstatic. Intimacy has no barrier in the divine world. As we are one with our soul's presence we feel free to know the intimacy of the sensuous experience of union with the Divine.

Sexual energy and spiritual energy come from the same source. Sexuality is the way that we allow the eternal to most fully enter our body. The creative fire of sexuality ignites the fire of passion to fill your body with aliveness. Any aspect of you that is not invested in being wholly alive will balk, be afraid of, decline or avoid the sense of aliveness that comes with sexual experience, for aliveness may be equated with harm or danger at a soul level.

Separation's Voice in Sexuality

Loneliness and the desperate need to know connection of the heart gets translated into the physical urge to sexually connect with another. When these wounds of separation lead us, we magnify the patterns of separation within us and wonder why our sexual experience seems to bring on more pain than pleasure.

A sense of powerlessness can cause us to misuse power or take advantage of another. It can fill in for a sense of power where the powerlessness of separation is felt. Taking advantage of another because of a sense of disconnection, and longing to feel connected, shows up in the field of sexuality at many levels. It usually finds its match in those who unconsciously believe that the only way they will know connection is by being taken advantage of. It takes two to tango, two wounds of separation acting out together, in this drive to know connection. If divine connection is not in the equation, we will do what we think we must to feel connected to *something*.

As small children we may have felt a heightened sensation of aliveness when touching our genitals. That's a natural, physiological design inherent in the body, to keep our spiritual connection in the body intact and magnified. The surge of aliveness and increased connection was real, if connection was not already fully shut down in us. Then the patterns of separation shown to us by those around us in the name of shame, fear and misunderstanding may have begun to take over in our relationship to our sexuality, which enhanced our separation to Spiritual energy as a sexual energy. We lost track of spiritual union as the sensual, full-bodied aliveness of creativity and ecstasy that our sexuality was designed to embody.

If we were sexually abused, our ability to equate spiritual energy with sexual energy became confused or shut down. So our sense of aliveness of connection to the Divine had no place to clearly land in our sensual, sexual expression.

These are just a few of the myriad ways we lost sight of the primary beauty and potency for union in our sexuality. In essence, we betrayed the divine arc between infinite Love and its embodiment in our life, greatly diminishing the abundant resource of true aliveness we were designed to relish and magnify.

To heal the wounds of separation in our vitality of sensuality and sexuality simply requires us to be with the colors of separation that are brought to the foreground in us when we engage sexually. Remember that the aspects of us that are not feeling alive are longing to reunite with the Beloved and its passion and pleasure pulsing through us.

Our Beloved Body

When we are available to Spirit as infinite Love, and embody the qualities of Spirit that are valuable to us, our physical body will do its natural job to bring infinite Love to life in all ways possible. That is its purpose. We came to planet Earth to experience Spirit moving through the physical dimension to consciously create and experience life in its abundance. Nature, the animal kingdom and the mineral kingdom do an excellent, inspiring job at this at their levels of creation. Only we experience separation, creating struggle, disease and limitation in our physical experience of Spirit's expression.

Our body is the means to give Spirit physical expression. What an amazing opportunity we have in realizing this gift of Love in physical form here. On the flip side, when our body is not being fed by Spirit it suffers in direct proportion to our patterns of separation. Facets of emotional separation will eventually translate to the body and impact it. Our cells naturally hold emotional memory, whether it's trauma or joyful aliveness.

If the cells get overloaded by patterns of separation they begin to break down—life force is not available—and dis-ease of every kind ensues. We must awaken to the reality of how the wound of separation is behind *every* physical limitation. It is the limitation of life force that produces shortages that reflect in physical limitations. Disconnection erodes the fiber of our existence.

The immune system is a key ingredient for Spirit's engagement in the body. It is the system through which the sustenance of life force moves to fill all the glands and organs. That is why the immune system is so pivotal to our health. There seems to be a growing number of autoimmune disorders and a growing diversity of the population impacted by a weakened immune system. I can't stress enough how direct the impact of separation is on the immune system.

When the immune system breaks down it is crying out for the resources of authentic connection to life force. It has been fed by patterns of living beyond our means, abandonment, living outside ourselves and fears of all kinds, just to name a few dominant ones.

Did you know that a virus in the body is caused by a weakness in the immune system? Often there seems to be no way of knowing where these viruses come from, what they are made of, and how to treat them. But they do seem to relate directly to our system's weakness and its inability to give the body what it needs to function optimally. Viruses slip into these pockets of weakness, i.e., places holding a pattern of separation.

If a plant is not given sufficient sunlight and water for its needs, it withers and dies. So it is with the body. If we are not sufficiently connected and we do not have true sustenance, we wither and die, either from emotional symptoms of withering that cause us to give up on life, or through physical maladies or accidents. There is a great degree of correlation between the increase in heart attacks and the increase in unhappy people creating lifestyles that are devoid of heart and soul nourishment. In some cases, it doesn't seem to matter how great your diet and exercise program is, if the heart is enslaved by fear, protection or patterns of shutdown, no amount of physical nourishment can get to it. If there is no opening to infinite Love, the truest level of nourishment is lacking and the body certainly cannot thrive without it.

Weight Issues

Weight issues are a very visible reflection of the wound of separation. Food seems to be the sole means for many to try to take in a sense of Love to fill the vacant places within us that are void of true aliveness. Control issues play into eating habits as well. Sometimes food is the only area where we feel in control of our well-being and means for getting our perceived needs met.

The following is a perfect example of the fact that the only true sustaining nourishment for aliveness and creation comes from Spirit. When we are available to the never-ending resources of infinite Love, our cells and, in this instance our digestive system, are not vacated or crying out for true nourishment, but truly smiling.

What is it I want when I reach for a piece of cake? Does the craving come from a part of me that longs to experience joy and believes that the cake is the only way I can connect with the joy and sweetness of life?

Food is meant to be a manifestation of Spirit's abundance. When we are connected to universal life force, the food we take in joins with that to nourish us the way the body, as an extension of Spirit, sees fit.

All the food we take in mixes with our energy field. If we are experiencing separation, food aligns with that separation and feeds further separation. The emotional pains build and accumulate. The body cries out in even louder pain, physically and emotionally. That scenario creates an even more desperate need for nourishment, mistranslated as false hunger or the need for more food. The problem grows instead of resolves.

There is a collective fear of running out of our essential resources of food, water and clean air. This fear is caused by the feeling of limitation and scarcity. This is a view from the separated perspective.

As we reunite with and claim the spirit of abundance and universal power and creativity, we know that resources will always be available. Spirit and form are one. Resources will be plentiful for those who cocreate with Source. Resources will abate if we live in fear. In the state of fear there is no available space to receive the infinite potential for creation. When we live as creators and providers of abundant life, we know we are taken care of and provided for.

I have worked with clients with such physical challenges as MS, cancer, lupus, chronic fatigue syndrome, candida, sports injuries and menopausal symptoms at the level of the soul. When we work with any issue at the level of the soul, we are healing the original cause for the pattern of separation that created the disturbance. There is always a direct correlation.[†] An effective, "permanent" success comes about in returning connection and life force to the area of need. The patterns dis-

---

† See my book, *Soul Radiance, Bring Your Soul Riches to Life.*

solve as each person experiences more value for their reunion with the endless possibilities of Spirit's gifts, such as Love, power, clarity, home, peace or stability, rather than valuing the pattern of separation held as disturbance.

About fourteen years ago, I went to the Mt. Hood, Oregon, area to assist six members of the U.S. snowboarding team to improve their performance levels in preparation for the Olympics. Each team member had a weakness in some part of their body that caused them to "cinch" up on various parts of their run. Coming out of the chute, one had his knees buckle. Another had legs that did not work optimally near the finish line. Another had a recurring weakness in the hip that would hold back her speed. The day after we worked together, each one reported that their snowboard run improved considerably. These young, dynamic athletes were not focused on their spirituality. I worked with them on the qualities of experience being sought after, which had been missing. Connecting with life force works in all situations regardless of our belief systems. The wounds of separation were unique to each athlete. The physical "hiccups" in their snowboard runs dissolved as they reunited and integrated each specific aspect with their inner strength of life force.

Feeling Limited

When we feel limited we are really saying that we do not feel free. Freedom is an inner state of being that contrasts with our state of feeling limited.

As souls, many have often felt that coming into a physical body has a confining sense of limitation. Many have perceived that the freedom of Spirit known by a soul in universal movement is somehow taken away when we move into a physical incarnation. The truth is that we choose to come into a physical form to expand our range of experience through the six senses. The outer world itself is filled with the endless possibilities but this capacity will only be appreciated if Spirit ignites our experience. It is our separation from the field of creation that leaves us feeling that our physical experience is barren and limited.

It is much easier and freer to reclaim our aspects that do not feel free and to reunite them with the freedom inherent in the vast field of Spirit than to continually avoid uncomfortable situations in order to feel a sense of possible freedom. Avoiding situations is a powerless and helpless place to be. The only way to truly know freedom is to be connected to the field of limitless possibilities. This field taps us into an expanded sense that all of creation is supporting us. This field, when we bring it into our body and especially into our creative power center that resides in our abdomen, is essential to our ability to feel empowered to fly freely in our life. As we connect to the anchor of universal freedom and our sense of creative power within, we feel limitless in what we can experience. We are then ready to freely create in any moment; our physical body is not seen as a limitation if it is filled with the gift of Spirit's wealth.

We are always faced with the challenges brought on by physical, emotional or mental patterns of separation. As we connect with Spirit in those aspects of ourselves and know the union of wholeness to a greater degree, we bring our soul to the soul of the planet, the soul of the universe and the soul of the field of creation.

7

THE WAY HOME

There is no valid reason to feel anything but happy, healthy, abundant and successful in all of our life. It is always a choice. As is the other choice: to be victim to our states of separation. Being a spiritual being in the human dimension certainly has its challenges. But we are moving out of the paradigm of putting all our attention on healing our wounds of separation. We are in a time of resourcing and reuniting with Spirit. To focus on reuniting with Spirit in the ways I have been describing throughout this book, rather than focusing on the lacks, the limitations, the wounds of separation, is simpler, more effective and powerful in its outcome. That is the way home.

Healing has been the modality we were ready for and could handle to this point in our collective pattern of seeking to be whole and connected. Now your connection to Love and Spirit is your catalyst and guide for life; the universal principles of manifestation begin to appear as daily miracles. As it should be! This is your time to know the beauty and splendor of being alive, part of the creative process that is the nature of life. You are quickly and gracefully gaining the tools and means to bring all aspects of your divine expression into wholeness.

The Return Home

Home is the word I am using to describe the foundational space we create within ourselves to welcome Spirit. It is also the sacred space we create so there is a trustworthy place within us that our aspects of separation can rest in so they can reunite with Spirit. Your sacred heart and soul rest in this sacred place that is uniquely yours.

> **Home is a place that is yours alone; in that place you are not alone.**

When you are in this home base you are connected to the universal home that your soul has always known and been a part of. The Creator exists in this universal home. You were born as a soul in this space of universal home. There, you came into individuated form and into human form, while you maintained the sanctity of your home connection to universal home. Home is your sanctuary and home base. It is where your knowing of infinite Love meets your capacity to embody Love and oneness in the human dimension. Moving out of separation begins with establishing this home base in yourself.

The Value of Home

On the journey to embody Spirit there are many valuable resources to help release fear and ego, and to clear blocks. Sometimes this task of clearing and repatterning can feel endless. Other times it's full of doubt. How do I know that what I am bringing in is aligned with Love and the greater dimensions of Spirit? Is it trustworthy? Is what I am connected to an imposter?

> **Your eternal self is helping you by presenting the perfect situations for you to bring those abandoned parts of you into reunion with your eternal self for your fulfillment in life.**

Each time more of you is brought back to reunite with its true home in connection to the eternal universal home you are, you know a greater sense of freedom, completeness and fulfillment. As you reach for greater connection to All That Is, you access these larger dimensions and embody them so that the field of creation can have an access point through you to this world. This is why you came. This is how you are of service. The whole universe is in this project of bringing this world into reunion with creation. As we connect to this field we can walk with confidence and a deep sense of foundational support into the myriad of experiences that unfold in our life.

Home Base Helps Us Navigate into the Unknown Future

There is no such thing as the unknown in the eyes of the Divine. When we hold a sense of oneness in our heart, when we embody oneness, we are guided by oneness. Our inner sense of holding oneness or Love is the known—always. From this perspective there is no unknown. We move into all new experiences from the known of oneness and Love. Through this, life is a great adventure of continual exploration. It is only our fear born from our sense of separation from the Divine that creates the sense that we don't know what is up. Our soul knows what we are up to. It holds the wisdom and clarity we need to further our creative pulsation of life expression. Limitless life resources are always available, even when some we thought were necessary to our existence fall away. These resources fell away, like the horse and buggy when cars came along, to make room for others that were more suited to the times we are in. With the tsunami in Indonesia a few years ago, much was washed away. At the same time a new species of plant life emerged that had never been seen before. Even more importantly, the massive destruction and loss of life brought fresh ways of seeing the gift of life. Evidence shows that new resources are always surprisingly available as we open ourselves to the larger fields of cocreation existing outside our fearful, restricted mind-sets.

> **Do not focus on how to serve the world. Ask yourself what makes you feel alive and embody that. This world is served by those who are alive.**

Embracing the Wound of Separation

The barnacles on the soul have created tangible patterns of separation that have traveled to be part of our personality and our way of walking in life. Now, with greater awareness of these patterns and how to identify them, you can take steps to accept them. Let them reveal themselves through you. Then you give these patterns the golden opportunity to know reunion and homecoming.

Anything that does not feel like the expression of our heart and soul is a sensation, emotion, pain or discomfort calling out from its place of separation to know reunion with its true home base. As you embrace this facet of your longing to come out of separation, it is vital to know that your divine self, as awareness, is witnessing this outcry of separation. It is bigger than the part that is calling out. It is present and must keep that perspective to assist this facet reuniting with Spirit through connection first to your home base within.

> **I am in command of my life. My body, mind and feeling realm are the field of my creation.**

You must first establish connection with the facet that wants to come home. Embody that connection and feel or see its presence within you. It must be real. This separate part only cries out when it knows there is a place in you to come, available to embrace it in its sensation of being separate from life force.

When you are feeling frustrated that you can't connect as deeply as you want, see that that sense of powerlessness comes as an opening, not a constriction. The energy of anger propels us to want what we don't have. That feeling of wanting can be elevated to a sense of conviction about connecting more deeply. You can feel how anger can be transformed into passion, which emanates from the belly, when that anger is connected to the longing of your heart and soul to be more than you have allowed yourself to be.

You may be feeling a sadness in relationship to the feeling of separation. That is the right starting point. Let the sadness of not feeling connected move to a heart longing to be connected.

Your inner place of connection, known especially through the soul and sacred heart, create a safe sanctuary for the return of this sacred, yet separated, aspect of you. As you hold your connection absolute and holy, the separated part of you will easily find its way into union with the eternal self. It will come easily of its own accord, choosing to be part of the light you have and hold. It will be ready to let go of its old job and create a new one as it integrates into your Spirit's embodied creative field.

When you know that, it is possible to connect with your inner guidance system and resources for infinite creation while a part of you is locked in fear or any other form of separation. You can do whatever is possible to move out of this fiercely limiting state.

> **Love yourself enough to give yourself and every precious part of you the gift of union.**

Connection for Our Separateness

To allow the separate aspects of yourself to find their way home, you must first connect to Spirit and infinite Love in the way that is most natural for you. It can be a visual image, an impression, a sensation, a color or a symbol of Spirit's riches that your heart and soul resonate with. The look or feeling of connection will also change and expand as you create from a larger sense of connected wholeness. Remember the hourglass theory to expand our field of creative influence in our world; we must expand the foundation of resources that are vital to that expansion in and through us. Let the nature of what describes connection for you be organic, and make sure it is authentic for you.

The next, most important, phase is to embody that connection, to make it real. That means breathing that quality of connection that is true for you into your heart. Let it be part of your heartbeat and bloodstream. Whatever it is that allows you to feel connected, let your sacred heart know its presence. This connection may change in its look when it arrives in the heart. That is natural. This embodiment of connection is key. The aspect of separation longing to have a home base to return to must find it within you. It is not enough for it to reach to some God energy, or universal place of peace beyond you. The return home is through your sacred heart and its connection to the universal heartbeat that you know as the peace of divine connection.

You are allowing this separated part to return to the eternal space of home that has always been present. Our soul has always resided in that blessed space of infinite Love and wisdom. Now you are opening to allow your whole self and life experience to be held in that sacred home within your heart that is connected to the field of all creation.

Know Home Truly Exists

There are many barnacles of the soul that you may identify that can make you feel wary of returning to universal home or trusting the journey there. You may even feel that home doesn't exist for you or you don't deserve to know it. Remember, it is only a facet of you that doesn't already know the depth of satisfaction of being home. That is the part that gets to be guided through this process of reuniting with home.

If you feel you have no sense of what it means to be connected to a larger sense of home, you are not alone. Now, in 2010, the housing market in the United States is out of control. This is symbolic of the fact that we have individually and collectively lost our true place of home.

Many homes are being taken away from families by the banks or mortgage companies they belong to. This situation is reflective of the fact that we have asked others to provide a home for us, which we are not capable of generating for ourselves. Living beyond our means in this instance relates to not knowing home internally, so we have been drawn to acquire houses and properties we can't pay for to give us the sense of home we long for. We feel hostage to banks and mortgage companies when we ask them to make a sense of home base possible for us.

As we rest assured within ourselves that we dwell in the beauty and universal peace and comfort of home, we can be creative in producing a physical reflection of home for ourselves. We can then extend the hope and strength that knowing an authentic connection to home provides to others wanting the same thing.

Home Within

True home is the place within us that knows all is well. It holds the union of the sacred heart and our soul. This home space thrives when you surrender to the larger field of universal home that exists. When facets of you are crying out in readiness to move out of separation to your home base, they will be happy to shift their allegiance from separation, if true home resides in you.

So often our spirituality consists of feeling moments of higher states, in meditation, or in nature, or in group settings, or with spiritual teachers. These states often feel separate from our outer life. Sometimes you might feel like you are leading two distinct lives.

Soul reunion is about embodying the qualities of Spirit we value in our life. This creates an ever-expanding home base for you to live from. Holding this place of home within you is vital so that separated facets have a real place to come to. Our facets of separation will not find peace or desire to integrate when we are blissed out from the neck up, but the rest of our body is feeling disconnected and homeless. There must be receptor sites within us for infinite Love to spread into our presence. And these same receptor sites must be a container and a home for Spirit. Then our separated parts can reunite with and know connection to all that is profound, expanded, and about being in the largeness of the field of Spirit. Through our internal embodiment of home, our wounds of separation can reclaim their connection to the ever-present Spirit that we are.

Allowing our connection to Spirit to live within us is certainly the key to our fulfillment. It is not enough to know peace as a higher, out-of-body state. As we bring Spirit's wealth of resources through our soul's connection to our heart, our separated parts will have a trustworthy foundation for their return to wholeness.

There are many methods for letting your connection to Spirit resonate within you. Be creative in making that bridge your priority and your fulfillment process will be greatly expedited.*

> **Our union with infinite Spirit quenches any thirst, any hunger.**

Authentic Surrender

When you surrender to the absolute connection to Spirit that your soul knows and trusts, your separated parts can begin to be released from their bondage. Your absolute connection to Spirit residing as a home base within you establishes a divine beacon in yourself for all aspects of you to move toward. You are reclaiming the stance that knows you are not alone; your life is divinely guided and you are choosing cocreation.

Surrender is not giving up or giving in to anything that you are not in command of. True surrender does not mean that you are at the beck

---

*My book *Soul Radiance, Accessing Gifts of Your Soul*, and the accompanying CD meditation, gives you great tools for connection to your soul essence. This includes the process of embodiment of all the qualities of Spirit you wish to create from life.

and call of something outside yourself, as though you are at the end of a string being pulled by some God that already runs your life. To surrender, for some, may feel as though they are going to that place of giving away yourself *again*. Surrender is about letting go of your survival grip, your willpower, your tendency to hold on to the side of the pool. To truly surrender requires that you know what you are surrendering to; it is real and has value and resonates in your heart. Embodiment of knowing connection within you allows you to feel safe to surrender to the expanded sense of what you value and what has sacred meaning to you.

What's at Risk

Ask yourself, what is at risk for you in opening yourself to your soul's connection to infinite Love and all of creation? When you honestly ask that question, it's a sure way to open the door for your separated parts to speak of their fears of surrendering to new, unknown or perceived unsafe dimensions. These parts speak through physical sensation, feeling sensation, mental chatter of all kinds. It is valuable to learn how your aspects speak to you. Then to learn how to listen, truly hear, and know how to guide home those previously left out parts.

What is at risk in giving these fears and pains the opportunity to regain connection to their True North? We would not be so afraid to meet, acknowledge and be with the pain that separation brings if we understood that this expression of pain comes from that part of us that is giving a signal that it is ready to be reconnected and fed by Spirit again.

To understand that the pain is there as a cry for help rather than just a reminder that you are suffering is truly freeing. It is vital to reframe our relationship to physical or emotional pain.

This process of reunion starts by holding compassionate understanding for that aspect of you wanting the assistance that you inherently hold, for you are infinite Love. This Love that you are resides in every atom within you, except for those places you have chosen to withhold from light.

Isn't it natural to want to give every aspect of yourself, residing outside of Spirit's strength and grace, what it longs for? We wish that for others; now we know how we can give that to ourselves.

Knowing that you have exactly what this blessed part of you is longing for is indeed fulfilling.

Rather than feeling debilitated, depressed or overwhelmed when these fearful parts in separation reveal themselves, you can declare in yourself that you know the way home and know how to assist that part in reclaiming its full potential. We may feel the pull of overwhelm when fears vividly present themselves. Do not give up on that part of you that seems to be hopelessly shutdown. It was given a choice around its position previously. You gave it its stance or viewpoint. Now it is asking to have a choice in its function and is requesting reunion with Spirit through you. For you to deny it, or not give it the opportunity for reconnection, is only saying to this aspect that you are closing the door to its way home.

When the sun shines in the morning it outshines the stars. The sun represents light and the stars represent our points of view, our ways of looking at things. There is nothing wrong with our points of view, or our states of pain and confusion. We just want to let the sun shine upon them and see what transpires when it is present in the realm of our stars.

A New Job Description

When certain aspects of you speak from their place of feeling limited, you can view these parts as department heads that are bringing the report of their internal perspectives to you. These parts were given a job by us. They are reporting to us how the job is going for them.

If they are showing up with emotions of fear, helplessness, anger or sadness, you can be sure that there is dissent in the ranks. You are getting the signal that the job is not working for them. Those parts are disconnected from infinite Love. Without connection, they will surely run out of creative juice and begin to complain. Be glad that you are on hand with the wisdom to know these parts are not happy with the job you gave then. This job was most likely based on protection or fear of being hurt so you would not have to feel abandoned, betrayed or rejected. Now you know they are simply mired in the pain of separation and want a new job assignment or description that is aligned with light, not fear, to bring you greater success and wholeness.

When you have opened the door for a part of you to reunite with Spirit, it may be a bit apprehensive at first. It may be drawn to or even love the idea of reunion but not be fully ready to make this leap of faith. Appreciate this aspect of you for the work it has done to this point at your request, keeping you shut down, small or even hidden. You asked this part to do this for you. Now you are asking it to have a new job description. You are expanding in your connection to infinite Spirit and this aspect is asking to come with you. This part has "heard" you for years saying you wanted it to keep you out of perceived danger or heartache.

Now you are expanding into a whole new way of being, and because you want to be whole and more alive, you are asking for a new way of participating from this aspect. It longs to be with you but may be skeptical about your trustworthiness or authenticity. You have gone back and forth in your head many times, wanting abundance but wanting to stay small. Wanting to share Love, but not wanting to get your heart hurt. Wanting to feel free, but afraid of the cost of freedom. This sacred part of you needs to know you are truly committed to your conviction to bringing forth abundance, Love or freedom.

It's like having asked a child for years to look both ways and hold your hand carefully while crossing the street because it's a dangerous world out there. Now you are essentially telling this child, with a grown-up body, that it is free to fly as it chooses. Of course it wants to fly. That is what it was born for. But it's been conditioned through repeated messages of caution and fear to do otherwise. Be compassionate, be gentle, but be true to your inner North Star so that these parts, longing to fly and assist you to create freely and abundantly, can have a graceful time coming on board with your vision and heart's desire.

You might ask yourself, who are you working for when you are creating a new experience of yourself and life? And who or what is that part in separation working for? I suggest that this part is asking to work for your heart and soul: for Spirit. You, as the CEO of your company, have exactly what any unhappy part wants or it wouldn't be coming to you for the answer to its need or complaint. When you are connected in your soul and Spirit, you are connected to the field of all creation. Creative solutions abound there for you to draw from.

The Process of Reunion

What does it feel like to be you? What you are sensing in your emotions or your physical body? Bring your attention to the crux of what is up for you, calling for your assistance. It is asking to be seen, understood, unlocked and transformed, so it is essential that you let yourself go right into it, to fully be with it. It can only be connected again if you let yourself experience it for what it is, in the fullness of its longing, in the fullness of the color of separation it is holding for you. Accept it with Love. Bring your awareness into it from the larger perspective of connected you. Remember, this feeling is something that you created. You asked a part of you to hold a certain job or position. You created it to punctuate the fact that you felt abandoned or rejected and you never want to feel that way again. So that part has been held in the place of separation you created for it, on your behalf. Also, it is asking to be freed up to assist you in creative ways, to come out of survival, or protection, or ego agenda.

Bring to your senses the nature of what connection looks like. The look of that connection changes throughout our life as we grow and expand spiritually. A picture of the sun, or the sensation of its warmth brought into your sacred heart can be a simple, sufficient embodiment of eternal Spirit within you. Your connectedness held within you is key.

It is a beacon of the light of home base being held within you for your separate aspect to reunite with.

Feel what is calling for your attention. Hear that aspect's words. Feel what you are feeling in that particular part of your body. See an image showing itself to you, or sense the sensation of discomfort, limitation or constriction. Remember, you chose the role that aspect is playing for you. This was the assignment and is the highest, truest way that aspect knows how to be.

Be with that aspect. Remember that you are connected to life, witnessing this aspect in separation. You might take the stance or make the following statement, "I am Spirit or infinite Love feeling ..." This helps you to avoid the feeling that the "cry for help" is you. It is just an aspect of you. When you see it this way it also helps you to bypass going into helplessness, powerlessness and hopelessness around having this feeling of separation. Hold the place of connected witness for this part that is feeling safe in your presence to reveal itself. Know that this aspect of separation's appearance means you are ready to let it stop running your life. Its cry is merely saying it wants connection and trusts you to provide it.

The you that is your soul essence, your divine essence, is present. That is why this aspect is calling out. It knows that you are present and connected enough at some level for it to know reunion and thus expand your sense of wholeness and abundance. This allows that part to feel safe to come forward and be heard and have the opportunity to be brought back to its original purpose for being.

Let this aspect that is suffering from separation declare itself in whatever way is natural for it, just as you would listen to a child, friend, partner or family member. Just as you would love to be heard, loved just as you are, in your weakness as well as your strengths. You are the power of Love that can calm any perceived storm.

You can ask "it" what it needs, wants or is lacking, even if it only presents itself as a sensation or constriction. Do not be afraid that you will be less loved or less connected to others that matter to you if you return to being more of your authentic self. As you become more authentic and abundant, you will be a greater magnet to those who genuinely appreciate you. You will feel a sense of deeper belonging to the world of Spirit, and connection to those in the world who honor infinite Love as you do. You are opening a space of validation for each part that presents itself to you. You are valuing it. Maybe this is the first time it has felt valued in a very, very long time.

Dance with the fear, embrace the feeling, for it is a vital part of you. See it as a child needing to be swept up in the arms of a parental sense of safety and knowing that all is well.

The Longing for the Experience of Spirit

Now ask that part, from your heart and soul: What are you crying out for, what do you long to connect to? You will discover that it is qualities of Spirit that this part of you is feeling separated from that it longs to reunite with. Maybe that fearful part wants nurturing support it never felt it could have. Or that aspect of you may be longing to reconnect with confidence and assurance, which is a quality of Spirit birthed from our innate connection to Spirit's natural fortitude.

If you say you are wanting to know a greater abundance, for instance, first notice what aspect of you, or where in your body, you are feeling a fear or doubt that this is not truly possible for you. Then ask that part what it needs. Does it need connection to infinite Love that will unconditionally support it as it grows to believe in itself? Does it wish for the support of Spirit's confidence that all is well and there is a place of purpose for you? Does it wish to connect to the field of all creation that reminds it that anything is possible in God? Does it simply wish to feel it has not been abandoned, and you, as eternal presence, never left it?

Open your heart and soul to listen to and be with this precious part of you that wants to know how to find its way home.

Then you might say to that precious part of you, "What else do you need?"

You can come to the listening place of your heart and soul very easily even when this cry from feeling separation appears deafening. You do this by putting your attention on something or someone you Love or appreciate. Sense the heart opening that occurs, even if it is subtle. The heart is the doorway to union with the universal All That Is. This heart in us is the sacred heart, not the human heart. I speak much more about the sacred heart in Chapter 3.

Your heart is now open as a receptor site for this aspect to come home to from the land of separation. As you bring whatever this separated part reveals to you back to the heart, as home base, it can be reunited with the nature and quality of what you know to be sacred. Remember, how connection looks or feels is unique to you. You can now begin to show this aspect that has been held in separation new possibilities for its expression of Spirit. This is key to remember. You are bringing home this aspect that has been suffering, to return to being an expression of Spirit. That is the greatest gift you can give yourself.

If you are a visual person, you might see that separated part and have an image of what connection looks like for you. If you are kinesthetic, you might feel the pain of that aspect that is feeling separate. You might feel your heart receiving that aspect and uniting with it as a simple welcoming, nurturing or strengthening sensation.

You might be auditory and hear what that separated aspect wants to say to you. You might work in a combination of these ways and create your own dynamic experience of the process of reunion. However it reveals itself for you, the key in this connection is the creation of a new compass of spiritual guidance for this aspect of you that has felt lost in its state of disconnection.

Hold the perspective throughout the process that you are cocreating with Spirit in this transformation and reunion. You could phrase this by encouraging those aspects that have been bound in separation. "We can do this."

We are molting the old and learning how to fly again. I celebrate any way that this reunion can transpire for you.

You are not only giving these separated facets of you what they long for, you are giving your heart and soul what they long for, which is the expanded expression of eternal you.

The *Ho'oponopono* Prayer

This ancient Hawaiian practice of reconciliation and forgiveness can be used quite simply and powerfully with the aspects of us that have been held in separation. As we remember that we were the one that chose to have this part of us be used as protection, defense or as a wall to keep us from being hurt, we will be more compassionate in helping this aspect to return home to the wholeness we are expanding into.

Speak the following *Ho'oponopono* prayer to that part longing to know reunion:

"I'm sorry.
Please forgive me.
I love you.
Thank you."

Then you open the door for this aspect to be with you, connected in Love.

The Gift of Reconnecting

First, you will be wholeheartedly with the beloved part of you crying out. Then you will put your attention on the resources of spiritual connection that are real to you. This resource could appear as a visual, as a word or sound, as a feeling or sensation, or a spiritual presence. This could be a symbol, such as the sun, a picture from nature or a celestial image. It could be the energy of an archangel or Spirit guide that you value. It could be the qualities of Spirit that a person, or mentor, holds for you. It could be a color. The possibilities are endless. Be open to how Spirit shows itself to you.

Now you will embody that resource by holding it in your heart or around your heart, or around you. Let it be real viscerally, so it has a sensation of being a part of you and your home base. You might feel or see an umbilical cord of connection to the spiritual quality you are connecting to, that shows up beyond you at first. Then you can breathe in that quality to connect it to your sacred heart so that it might now live there.

You might also see two cords plugging in to each other, as though the power is being switched on again between Spirit and your separated part. Maybe you are plugging in that aspect of your self to a wall socket to turn on and to get creative power moving into it again. Let your creative imagination find its way in opening you to your resources for spiritual connection that allow this particular aspect of your longing for reunion to be fulfilled.

Then let that aspect join with you in reunion, in whatever way is natural for this particular moment of its homecoming. When you bring the sensation of emotional or physical pain in the body to the sacred heart, you can use your breath to bring them together. Let this breath be a deeply connected breath that reaches to the stars, anchors your divine connection, then brings those resources to your heart with your breath. Then breathe that fullness into and around the separated aspect of you longing for this infiltration.

Knowing Reunion

The main ingredient to be known in the process is the sensation of reunion that occurs. It is a true homecoming over and over again. Welcome the electric, the warm, the soothing, the satisfying or the powerful energy that occurs. Allow it to move into your body. The sensation of expansion, strengthening, Love, peace, wholeness and coming together may be accompanied by tears of joy, relief, reunion and satisfaction. The sense of greater aliveness and freedom, and wanting to engage even more deeply and vibrantly in life, is exhilarating. The sense of overriding peace can be palpable. You may feel a more subtle sense of any of these qualities of experience. Just know that the more you allow yourself the gift of participating in this process of reunion, the greater the sense of fulfillment you will know; the more on purpose you will feel.

The Universe is deeply grateful for every aspect of you.

Spiritual Drano

The universe and its ability to pour forth its gifts through you will expand each time you give yourself the gift of blessed reunion. To feel at home in your own skin as part of a majestic expression of Spirit is the fulfillment you have been looking for and can now attain, over and over.

Wouldn't you much rather have Drano when your drain is clogged, than to have to reach down and pull out every part of the clog, piece by piece? Yuk. The clog is the voice of "I don't know. I can't. I'm afraid. I'm angry. I don't trust. I'm grieving a loss." These are voices of the victim clogging your flow to reunion. All these clogs create constriction to Spirit's movement in you.

You can see this process I am describing as spiritual Drano. We are bringing the hand of Light into the area of need, and lifting it up as the old way of functioning is simply washed down an energetic drain. Space is created for the clear water of life to move again through what was constricted and is now expanded, bright and shiny.

It is much simpler to bring in connection to what you long for than to try to keep clearing the pattern you don't want. I see it as the theory of displacement or replacement. When you bring into the area of separation what truly makes your heart sing, the old pattern simply dissolves.

You will notice when you move those disconnected parts back into the light of day that life for you is brighter and you walk with a lighter step. These resources you have just created, by bringing aspects of yourself out of darkness or shadow to connect to the light of day, will be resources that allow you to live the abundant ways you are designed to. You are allowing those clogs in your drain to shape-shift into nourishment for your Spirit to know expansion of Love, joy, success and a deep sense of purpose.

Everything in life is connected to all creation. We are traveling in a physical reality where everything has already been created energetically. That energetic reality is absolutely supported and empowered. You can bring all those aspects of yourself that are presently moving from a weakened, powerless, unsupported state of existence to this home that lives in the field of all creation.

As we expand into this reality that we are infinite Love and Spirit, in all aspects of ourselves, there is no unknown to traverse. We walk as Love, we go to our job as Spirit creating in the world, we relate to those in our world as fellow beings in the adventure of life. We hold the knowing that all is well in the universe of our creation and know we will magnetize, out of that field of creation we are, all that we need as Love embodied here. Our connection to universal presence is our true anchor, our only security, the true safety net.

This time on the planet is calling us not only to remember, but know, and be the beloved creators that we are in our wholeness of being in the physical dimension for its expression.

The secret to healing is actually found in moving beyond the level of healing. When we focus on healing we are focusing on the mind-set that there is something to fix. When you expand to the higher dimensions where the healed state dwells and bring those higher dimensions to be embodied within you, the transformation naturally occurs. It is a law of nature. The old place of separation is replaced by Spirit's infusion. It does not have to be healed, it is transformed in its reunion with Spirit as its guide.

We are simply dying to our ways of disconnection in our life, and giving birth to a richer, freer, more joyful expression of life radiantly pouring through us.

We are reclaiming life over death in those areas we choose to resuscitate, as we create a partnership with the Divine instead of with separation.

Home as Connection to Our Spiritual Family

The return home from separation already lives within us. If you are feeling fear, defeat, powerlessness, grief or frustration, take a moment to contact the connected aspects of yourself. This could be the aspect of you that knows you are a great teacher, or that knows your ability to do a job well, to cook, love a dog, smell a flower, run a mile. These may look like things you do, but they are qualities of expression that dwell in you even when a feeling based in separation steps up to the plate.

Make a circle for yourself, either on paper or as a mental image, of these aspects within you that are alive and well, those places in you where you can still feel light coming through. Let that circle of shining attributes be part of a sense of satisfaction in you, which is a quality of home. Then let this aspect of separation find its way to connect with that feeling of satisfaction within your circle that carries a sense of home. Let the circle encompass this aspect, remembering it is wanting to be witnessed and brought into the light. It is crying out for help to remove its self-created shell that it feels captured within. This shell makes this part believe that it doesn't belong. It feels isolated, alienated and lonely. It feels it is being kept from expressing itself. It wants out of its seclusion. That is why it has stepped forward.

Let it be surrounded by the aspects of you that are connected and have light moving through them. Any amount will do. You do not have to be in an ecstatic state to hold the light of Spirit. Bring that separated aspect into the fold. Let it feel light again and have the opportunity to choose what it wants to align with. Does it want limitation or the freedom that comes with union with light?

You may see or feel a sense of home in yourself when you think of a family gathering, or a gathering of people you love to be with. You may also see home base acquainted with a group or a circle of people, beings or souls that represent spiritual family to you, as a valuable aspect of home. If this is the case, bring your separated part into this circle. When you are opening the door for its reunion with Spirit, let it be held by the circle, transformed by the circle, or uplifted by the circle. Or it might join with the circle, merge with it, become one with it. Let it be there until it feels at home and one with the larger self which this family represents. In essence this circle is saying, "You are wanted by life."

Push Your Refresh Button

When you are feeling "I don't want to be here" you can push the refresh button and rephrase that sentence. First say, "I don't want to be here like this, in this state of separation. I don't want to be in this state of separation I am in right now. I don't want to be here with this fear, or this overwhelming sense of loss, etc., that is a state of separation within me." That will begin the whole process of moving toward union again.

When we say, "I can't live like this," remember to say, "I can't live like this without connection to Spirit."

"I feel like I am dying." Push the refresh button and say, "I feel like I am dying without a true connection to Spirit right now."

If you need hope in relationship to anything in your life, let your heart take in a universal light and connect it to that idea or feeling that is lacking hope. Then infuse the part of you that feels hopeless with that light that represents hope in your heart.

In relationship to whatever you want, you can push the following refresh button: if you are declaring, "I want freedom," you are really saying at a deeper, authentic level, "I want the freedom that comes with connection."

What is it you want to be connected to in order to have something that you are wanting? For instance, if you say you want more money, ask yourself what it is you want to be connected to, which is usually a quality of Spirit, in order to have more money.

Example of the Return Home from Separation

Sylvia came to see me, with tears in her eyes and hope in her heart. To put it simply, she had adrenal exhaustion and menopause was taking it over the top. She spoke of her sense that she had virtually been in fight-or-flight mode all her life. She was happy with the supplements she was taking and the acupuncturist she loved, as well as her medical doctor who had given her sage advice. But she sensed there was a deep-level pattern that remained to be addressed.

I told her all the physical and even energetic assistance she was wisely receiving would also be greatly enhanced by resolving the soul-level issue of separation. As reunion and wholeness are returned, the supplements can fully do their job of supplementing the physical manifestation of the pattern of wholeness being reclaimed.

We spoke of her spiritual connection and what that meant for her. She got in touch with the resources of nurturing, supporting Love that was real for her. In that process, which I am not describing here, Glenda, the good witch from *The Wizard of Oz*, showed up. She carried the qualities of Spirit that Sylvia valued for Love and support of a somewhat maternal nature, a touch of queenliness and a portion of magical fairy.

Then I asked her to connect with a more masculine energy resource that represented assurance, confidence, strength and absolute connection to Love. The Greek god Zeus appeared. As we spoke together of her fight-or-flight pattern and her consequential physical symptoms, she kept Zeus and Glenda in her heart. Having them in her heart, and around her, made them a part of her and not just distant fairy-tale characters of her imagination.

Her fight-or-flight pattern resided primarily in her adrenals. She was somewhat aware of that but had never thought of seeing them as more than physical carriers of these patterns in need of greater hormonal support.

We took a journey to her adrenals to uncover what her wound of separation was about that her body insisted on carrying for her. We brought Glenda and Zeus to hold loving support for her so that the adrenals felt safe to reveal their cry for help. She realized that the fight-or-flight pattern itself was a constant cry for help, combined with a need to protect Sylvia at all costs from some form of danger. That protection from harm sounded like a reasonable job description. But then Sylvia put her attention more deeply on what the fight-or-flight pattern in her adrenals was about.

With Glenda's loving support and presence, she realized that her adrenals were on fight or flight to keep her from getting hurt in relationship to Love. That sounded smart. Then Sylvia broke down in tears and said that she felt her fight-or-flight mechanism was in place to keep her from *all* Love, so she wouldn't get hurt. That was going overboard. Somehow the phrase "it's not safe to love here" leapt out. Deep in Sylvia's memory was this message that it is not safe to be connected to Love here and she had hired her adrenals to uphold that belief. Love = danger, so we must be on fight or flight continually to keep Love out. That painful pattern felt ancient to Sylvia. It made no sense to her consciously why she would shut out all connection to Divine Love. I explained to her how that works at a soul level. She understood and realized why she had such an internal struggle going with her relationship to everything she loved. It was as though she felt she didn't have permission at some unseen level to really know joy and abundance. She had a built-in mechanism keeping her from seeing these qualities as anything but dangerous!

We brought Zeus and Glenda to be with her adrenals. Sylvia realized they were messengers for divine Love. I had her connect to their presence of divine Love through her sacred heart to her adrenals and whole endocrine system. She pictured a divine syringe being placed by her adrenals, permanently injecting divine Love as an opalescent liquid. Her new commandment came to her in the following words: With Love I am safe. As I live as Love and feel held by universal Love, my adrenals have a new job.

The adrenals became in union with divine Love. They got a new job—to be a storehouse to make sure Love is available for any immediate need at hand. This Love injection would ensure that Love was called on as the first response to any call from the place of separation, mostly held as fear, that the body or emotional field might carry.

Sylvia promised to herself always to keep connected to Zeus and Glenda as her supportive representatives of connection to divine Love. And she continued to picture the divine liquid of opalescent light coming into her adrenals. This way she knew Love came with her wherever she went.

The Journey of Expansion from Home

Many of us who saw the movie *Avatar* felt recognition in our soul that the way life was lived on Pandora was very natural and real to us. It was a depiction of a remembrance of a divine state, a true way of being that our heart and soul knows still exists in essence for us. Let that possibility live in your heart and body, and it will appear at this level of creation.

As we allow those disconnected parts of us to awaken and reunite with our Spirit, the magnificence and splendor depicted in the realm of Pandora will emerge in the physical dimension for Spirit's expression that we came to embody.

When you are ready to let go of the illusion of separation and rise to the level of connection to all that is abundant and life-giving, you will see and experience relationship to this world very differently. You will move in the world from a place of union with all that is beloved. Your outer dimensions will expand continually into wholeness, given freely as your gift to the world.

Remember to love yourself enough to give every precious part of you the gift of union with universal Love.

**Reunion with the Divine is our purpose,
Embodiment of that union is our fulfillment.**

Resources

To contact Susann for a personal appointment, an Akashic Record reading, a Soul-Essence journey, a Soul Reunion session, a book presentation, to speak at an event or to conduct a workshop, e-mail her at susann@soulmastery.net.

Visit her website **www.SoulMastery.net** for a schedule of her workshops, teleseminars, trainings and teleclasses, and to purchase her books, CDs and DVDs.

Other Books by Susann Taylor Shier

Soul Mastery: Accessing the Gifts Of Your Soul

Soul Mastery gives you direct contact with your Soul family and its heritage. This very real and practical knowledge opens your heart to its deepest nature and purpose. Experience a sacred reunion with your Soul, and a positive, profound and joyful knowing of your true essence and gifts. Truly understand yourself and others from the viewpoint of Soul heritage. Discover the majesty of your Soul and be filled with joy for what you see. Come home to the gifts of your Soul.

Soul Radiance, Bring Your Soul Riches to Life

With *Soul Radiance* you will journey to your Soul-Essence to connect with the resources you need for soulful manifestation. Let your Soul connection guide you to ignite the change you long to create. Deepen communication with your Soul to engage wholeheartedly in the abundance of a Soul directed life.

ABOUT THE AUTHOR

Susann Taylor Shier presents Soul Mastery, Soul Radiance and Soul Reunion workshops, book events, trainings, and teleclasses. She has been featured on numerous TV and radio shows. She travels across the US and she works internationally as a psychotherapist and intuitive counselor with clients in person and on the telephone. Her first book, Soul Mastery: Accessing the Gifts of Your Soul was published in 2005. Her second book, Soul Radiance, Bring Your Soul Riches to Life was published in 2008.

She lives in Santa Monica, California.

Discover more about the author's work at
www.SoulMastery.net